Friendship, LLC

Copyright © 2012 Zachary A. Schaefer Ph.D.
& David J. Ponder CISA
All rights reserved.

ISBN: 1-4800-8208-2
ISBN-13: 9781480082083

Friendship, LLC

A Story of Laughing, Learning, and Childhood Shenanigans

Zachary A. Schaefer Ph.D.
&
David J. Ponder CISA

Dedication

To our parents and brothers, for helping us become decent people.
To our wives, for helping us remain decent people.
To our indecencies that led to laugher and success.

Table of Contents

Prologue
Chapter One–FIRST IMPRESSIONS 1
Chapter Two–Spontaneous Search Party 5
Chapter Three–Grade School Switcheroo 11
Chapter Four–CAUGHT IN THE ACT 19
Chapter Five–Extreme Truckers
 and Middle Fingers 21
Chapter Six–Antenna Removal Service 29
Chapter Seven–Prank Calls and Police 37
Chapter Eight–THINKING BIG 47
Chapter Nine–Hustling Our Way to the NBA 51
Chapter Ten–Magical Bartenders 59
Chapter Eleven–Pyramid Schemers 65
Chapter Twelve–RESPONSIBILITY HAPPENS 71
Chapter Thirteen–Boating, Bonding,
 and Cleaning 73
Chapter Fourteen–Guinea Pig City 79
Chapter Fifteen–Boxing, Brawling, and Bravery 89
Chapter Sixteen–Reflections and Perspectives 93

Prologue

Steak N' Shake Laser Show

After a long day of go-kart shopping in South St. Louis with my parents, my brother Justin, my best friend Zach, and his younger brother Josh, we needed to grab a quick bite to eat before heading back over the Mississippi river into Illinois. My dad gave us a simple choice: Steak N' Shake or McDonalds. That's a no-brainer for young boys. Anytime we ventured into St. Louis it was like a mini road trip. So we decided to wine-and-dine ourselves on the gourmet food at Steak N' Shake. They are, after all, "steak" burgers, not the maybe-beef patties that *Mc-What's-Their-Name* serves. Eating at Steak N' Shake was a wonderful experience and not just for the food. At Steak N' Shake, friendly workers actually greeted you inside, sat you at a table, and took your order. People enjoyed working there, unlike McDonald's workers who were about four years older than us and constantly had the "get me outta here" look etched on their faces.

The kids weren't the only ones who wanted to eat at Steak N' Shake. My parents loved this place too. Zach and I recognized why my parents fawned over the 1950s nostalgia at Steak N' Shake even if we didn't know what nostalgia meant. This restaurant transported them back to the "good old days" in the 1950s, the server's little red bow ties and checkered company logos created a *haute couture* atmosphere ('high culture' for you non-fancy folks) that persuaded my parents to avoid the sweat-covered indoor child playgrounds at McDonald's.

Zach and I ordered the exact same meal each time we dined at Steak N' Shake: one large order of golden, flawlessly fried potatoes, two double-stack cheeseburgers smeared with the proper amount of mustard to coat the entire top bun, with melted American cheese dripping over the rough edges of the steak burgers and perfectly placed pickles. We would also split a large chili for dipping our fries and burgers into. Seinfeld would not have enjoyed this meal, because we were habitual triple-dippers. We each finished the meal with a large hand-dipped, real milk chocolate shake. We envisioned a heaven where everyone drank chocolate Steak N' Shake milkshakes whenever they pleased.

On this particular dining experience, our waitress was a woman named Velma, or at least that's the name I remember her saying through her coarse, lifelong smoker voice. Velma was a grizzly veteran of the food industry. Instead of the smiling, polite, good looking waitress portrayed in Steak N' Shake commercials, this woman should've been working at a truck stop in a foreign wasteland. She clearly didn't take crap from anyone, especially four snot-nosed grade schoolers. Velma didn't realize, however, that Zach and I had recently purchased a new toy: a small laser pointer. She was clearly not prepared for what was to come. Please remember that this incident occurred years before any crazies actually started shooting people in public places. It was also before the days of idiots blinding pilots in plane cockpits, and we would never have considered something so dangerous. Well, at least we didn't think of the idea before becoming wise enough to know better.

This particular laser pointer was very powerful–you could see the bright red dot several hundred yards away, so using it in close proximity magnified the strength and density of the dot. It was also very compact, small enough to fit in the palm of your hand. As Zach was finishing up his second steak burger, he came up with a great idea. He wanted me to move the laser around the room and put it on customer's shirts who Velma was interacting with, so no matter where she went the laser would follow. It didn't take long. When Velma first noticed the red laser dot, she was carrying a tray with two milkshakes intended for the table next to us. Before we knew it, the red dot must have distracted Velma because she tripped and fell. The milkshakes beat her to the ground. The sound of crashing glass and the display of raw terror that came across Velma's face, which was partly covered in Vanilla ice cream, made for a horrifying scene. The humor involved in this situation quickly vanished. I immediately hid the laser inside my pants pocket and we spoke nothing of what happened inside the restaurant … but my parents were already onto us. We had been using them as guinea pigs for our laser treatments while driving around that day, and my dad was not happy.

Moral of the Story: Older, lifelong smokers carrying a tray of milkshakes may not have the stability and coordination required to withstand a 5-megawatt laser to the cornea. On a more serious note, we learned that small pranks can lead to unintended negative consequences. We never meant to frighten anyone, only to make them guess who was playing the prank. Dave's parents were not fans of our laser show, and they let us know by grounding us for two weeks and throwing away our laser.

Introduction

This is the story of an unintended lifelong friendship that developed while searching for a lost set of car keys. It is the story of two young boys growing up in the Midwest United States who, at an early age, learned to appreciate and apply the values associated with a Midwestern lifestyle. It is the story of how kids and adults need to focus on enjoying life, dreaming big, and working hard to fulfill those dreams. It is a story about how interesting outcomes emerge from spontaneous circumstances and how creative collaboration will always lead to a larger quantity and higher quality of ideas. This brief book traces the synergy that was formed the first night that the authors met each other and illustrates how we have personally and professionally benefitted from maintaining such a close friendship for so many years.

Zach Schaefer and David Ponder have been best friends since Don Schaefer moved next store to Art and Mary Ponder's house on South 5th Street in Belleville, Illinois, in 1991. Zach was eight and Dave was nine. There was something special about that neighborhood and the ten or so boys who grew up in it. We got into plenty of mischief, created lots of havoc for our parents, and at times, kept the Belleville police department busy, but we also learned important lessons that have defined who we are as friends, family members, husbands, and young professionals. We have written this book to share our stories, to encourage people to find a friend who can challenge them to move beyond their limits, and to document the process by which we became men. Even at an early age we knew that there were many types of "men" one could become—we had plenty of positive and negative role models in our neighborhood—and in all modesty, we feel that we became pretty good ones.

Albert Einstein said, "Try not to become a man of success but rather become a man of value." Although we did not consciously apply this wisdom in our everyday lives as boys, we have become men of value because of our close friendship and our willingness to hold each other accountable for the values, lessons, and goals encountered and appreciated throughout our journey. These values, lessons, and goals are sprinkled throughout the book. We have organized the book into four themes, and each theme has several relevant chapters that demonstrate the significance of each theme. You will recognize the themes because the words consist of all capital letters. We conclude each chapter with "Morals of the Story" to really drive home the lessons we learned. We recognize that most people don't read books anymore because they are too busy or they prefer to turn on the television, so we have kept our morals simple, brief, and clear in the hope that people can transfer some of our knowledge and lessons to their own lives. In writing our book, we wanted to try to understand the synergy we feel when we put our minds together to achieve a goal. We believe we can do almost anything in life, and we have been very happy with our choices to this point. To ensure that we each had a voice in the book, we switch the *perspective* in each chapter so that roughly half of the chapters come from each of our voices.

This book is for anyone interested in learning about how close friendships can transform your worldview and personality in a positive way. We highlight who we were and who we have become by collecting the formative stories engraved in us and our loved ones. In addition to discussing the benefits and pleasures of having a trusted companion to share ideas (and mischief) with and supporting each other's life decisions, this book debunks the myth that you shouldn't conduct business with friends. We have both started our own businesses and rely on each other to achieve our different professional goals.

Creativity means rearranging what you already know to transform the way you think about and view the world. Creativity is about ideas, but innovation adds an "action" component. Dave and I have created an innovative relationship that allows each of us to pursue our interests, challenges each of us to think beyond our current knowledge limits, and motivates each of us to do this in an ethical manner. Our goal is to add value to each other's lives, workplaces, professions, and society as a whole. By unintentionally (and luckily, in hindsight) developing a sense of responsibility during our childhood years, we are now one step closer to attaining an entrepreneurial mindset. We call ourselves personal and professional entrepreneurs—personal entrepreneurs in relationships and experiences, professional entrepreneurs in our breadwinning occupations and our passionate business creations. An entrepreneurial attitude is important to each of us because entrepreneurs are optimistic, persistent individuals who surround themselves with intelligent people. We realized early on that if you want to soar like an eagle, you can't surround yourself with turkeys. As fate would have it, we have found that symbolic creature in each other.

Creative Conversations + Entrepreneurial Actions + Societal Value = Friendship, LLC

Chapter 1
FIRST IMPRESSIONS

Nothing is as powerful in the realm of human relationships as a first impression. To paraphrase Oscar Wilde, humans never get a chance to repeat this opportunity. Within the first ten seconds of meeting someone, we make snap judgments about their personalities, beliefs, and character based on how they dress, what they say, and how they react to our greeting. These first impressions stick with us because we are constantly categorizing people, ideas, events, and objects. We automatically search for ways to simplify the world by relaying on heuristics—mental shortcuts such as trial and error—and stereotypes to make sense of the world and our relationships. Many first impressions occur in a split second during "chance encounters" with strangers.

The grocery checker, the coffee shop barista, the elevator-riding partner enter our lives for a moment and are gone just as quickly as they arrived. The interesting part of chance encounters is the huge impact they can have on our lives. Our close friends and significant others form the structure that our lives grow around, shaping and supporting us as we age. These chance encounters can change our lives in unexpected ways, and only in hindsight can we understand just how important meeting that stranger really was. Humans tend to think that they're experts at reading people and that first impressions are always spot on. We reason that the people in our lives are there because we identified them, picked them out of thousands of others based on our intuition.

Although serendipity plays a larger role in bringing people together than most people care to admit, some people are naturally good at reading people and getting along with a wide array of personalities. Society calls these social magnets "people persons." If you are a people person, you get along with most people in most situations. You are aware of the impression that you are making on others and pay attention to the impressions that others are making on you. Dave and I have always been judicious first-impressionists. I was a spontaneous, strong-headed child who disdained authority (not much has changed other than my rung on the ladder of authority). Although I was an independent child, I still liked to please others, I strived for personal recognition, and I continually sought social approval. Dave was also a people pleaser but took a different approach. He was a generous, benevolent, and introverted kid who enjoyed helping others and solving problems. The seeming contradiction of Dave's calm nature and my assertiveness helped create the ideal foundation for a solid friendship. Our first impression of each other grew out of a chance childhood encounter that allowed us to quickly establish our social roles in our relational dynamic.

Childhood is nothing more than an exercise in observing and understanding social roles. We learn by

Friendship, LLC

watching people get rewarded and punished for certain actions, and we also learn by personally being rewarded and punished. Dave and I preferred to do this "social learning" together if only for the reason that we would share in each other's rewards and punishments. As the saying goes, "Misery loves company," but we also learned that *shared laughter* is the best medicine. As kids figure out their roles, they begin to understand who they are and what they want out of life, and they begin to either work well or poorly with others. Dave and I quickly discovered our social roles in the context of our relationship: Dave was the classic nice guy who cared about others' feelings and enjoyed making people happy. He was confident and content but quiet. I relentlessly sought to make others laugh, and because I was small for my age, I exhibited "defensive dominance," where I would size people up and always have a smart-mouth comeback or a verbal assault ready to be unleashed. Dave's introversion was the polar opposite of my attention seeking. Out of this fusion of what I call sarcastic sincerity grew a form of collective decision making, in which Dave and I both developed confidence in ourselves—although in our own ways—because we were able to share our ideas, triumphs, and failures with a polar opposite. The following two chapters will share the beginnings of our friendship, and how those experiences, which appeared normal and mundane, changed the course of our lives forever.

Chapter 2
Spontaneous Search Party

Kids don't have adult baggage. No responsibility, no worries, no fear from self-consciousness. That's why they're experts at losing and breaking objects that have significance for other people. Kids also love doing things when they are told not to do them. It's that whole "forbidden fruit tastes sweeter" mentality that they haven't learned to suppress. Had I listened to my father and never disobeyed him, my friendship with Dave might not have blossomed into a lifelong brotherhood. Our first meeting and impressions of one other went something like this:

One evening, my Dad, brother, and I were pulling up to my Dad's new apartment in his full-length, red-and-white van with the license plate ZacJos2. My brother Josh and I loved riding around in Dad's van because we could crawl among the three rows of seats. It was like having a jungle gym built into your car. That's why all those seatbelt PSAs were created, and the child car-seat industry made millions exploiting good-natured people like my Dad. When my brother or I misbehaved, which was often, Dad would "reason" with us and try to explain why our actions were inappropriate.

Although it sounds useful, this strategy rarely produced the desired result, and in fact, my brother and I sort of enjoyed my father's speeches. We learned we could get away with a lot when we were with him as long as we looked remorseful and fearful when he gave us one of his "talks." A few times he had tried spanking us on the legs, but we would all start laughing—Dad included—during that punishment, so that was pretty much the end of that.

On this particular evening, my brother and I were in a rowdy mood from all the excitement of the move to the new duplex. We were looking forward to meeting new kids to run around with, and Dad was excited about the larger space and detached garage. My Mom and Dad got divorced when I was seven years old and Dad first moved into a real rat-hole of an apartment, so when he moved across the street from the Ponders it felt like we moved into the Taj Mahal. The new location was also down the road from our grade school, Cathedral, which meant Dad could take us to school, and we could spend the night with him more often during the school week.

As soon as we exited the "Don-Mobile" my brother and I started running around the front yard like chickens with our heads cut off. It was dusk and quickly getting dark, and all Dad wanted was to get set up inside the apartment. But I had other plans. Somehow, I ended up with the keys and decided to make a bet. (To this day I love making bets but I do not enjoy playing poker or casino gambling. My preference is for "silly" bets—on names, dates, or guessing a restaurant bill. I've always derived great pleasure out of winning, and silly bets allow you to turn any situation, no matter how mundane, into a potential "memorable winning moment." Looking back, all of my goofy bets make for great stories.) This particular bet, with Josh, was that I could throw Dad's keys into the air as high as possible and catch them as they came down. Adults would make the rational decision to keep the keys in their pocket for multiple reasons: (a) its dusk, (b) they're in uncharted territory, and (c) no one has a spare set of keys. Eight-year-old Zach was unfazed. I hurled those precious metal door-openers and car-starters into the air as high as I could. I was a pretty good baseball player and could throw the ball fairly well, and catch it, too. But this was no ball I was catching. My dad was not a janitor, but looking at his keys he might have been. I'm surprised he could even start the Don-Mobile with the amount of heavy metal hanging from the ignition switch.

I got ready for my first throw. I took a crow-hop and hurled the keys directly over my head, then with my brother, scrambled to catch them. Thump! Bulls-eye! I caught the first toss square in my palm, which damn near cut my hand open, but, what the heck, I was ready for another round. I turned to Josh and said, "Double or nothing I can throw the keys AND spin in a circle before I catch them." "You're on," he said. At this point Dad was telling me not to throw the keys again because it was getting dark, and he didn't have a flashlight handy to find them in the yard. Ha! Terrible advice! He just didn't know how to have fun and didn't recognize my eagle eyes and superior hand-eye-coordination.

This time I threw the keys so hard I thought I threw my arm out of socket. I spun around not because I wanted to but because the throw had contorted my body. Josh watched in half horror and half delight. He knew he was going to win the bet but realized not only that I could hurt myself but that we would both be in trouble if I lost those keys. If the sun were a little higher in the sky, I might have been able to capture a glint off the keys' metallic surfaces, but as it was I was staring at the blank canvas of a dark-blue sky. Uh-oh.

I lost sight of the keys as soon as they left my hand, and unfortunately Josh was watching me and not the precious payload. We had no clue where they landed because I was groaning about how badly I had hurt my arm. As soon as Dad realized what had happened, Josh and I envisaged a return to the spankings, only in a slightly more, shall we say, aggressive manner.

Lucky for Josh and me, we had very understanding parents. Sure, Dad yelled a bit and guilt-tripped me into feeling bad, but this night there were no real repercussions, other than my having to look for the keys on my hands and knees for roughly an hour in the dark. I later thought this would have been an excellent punishment for prisoners because it was obvious the damn keys were never going to be found. This thought occurred to me when, during a tour of Alcatraz many years later, I learned that prisoners in solitary confinement would rip the buttons off their shirts, toss them in the air, and then crawl around their pitch-black cells searching for the buttons to pass the time. This was to keep them from going crazy from sensory deprivation.

Friendship, LLC

I performed this same exercise to keep my Dad from going crazy from sensory overload.

Unbeknownst to us, the family across the street was watching this awkward moment with great curiosity as the four of them—two adults and two sons, who, I would soon find out, were about the same age as Josh and I—rocked slowly and silently on their front-porch swing. For the entire hour of my crawling around on all fours, they sat on that damn swing without so much as an offer of help, just enjoying the cool summer evening. Later, Dave would insist they were never on the front porch in the first place and certainly wouldn't have sat on that swing for an hour while a family man's sons scoured the earth for keys. (I disagree with your recollection, Dave, and this is my chapter.)

Finally, Art said, "Enough is enough" and walked his family over to help us find the keys. He brought flashlights and we found the keys within five minutes, due largely to Dave and his brother Justin crawling around our yard on their hands and knees, right alongside my brother and me. Dave literally got down on his hands and knees to help another person, without expecting anything in return, the stuff of which friendships are born.

The search had taken so long because the keys had lodged themselves underneath one of the van's tires on the side facing the street. During the search introductions were made and banter exchanged: where did you go to high school (for our parents)? What parish do you belong to? Where do your kids go to school? What sports do you play? Josh and I got excited about having neighbors our age, who played the same sports we did, and who were cool enough not to make fun of me for losing my father's keys and being forced to participate in a "spontaneous search party" on an otherwise perfect summer night. Even though I lost the bet with my brother, I gained a best friend. It was one of those intensely satisfying moments where a "win-win" emerged from a chance encounter.

Morals of the Story

1. Silly bets can turn normal situations into amusing, interesting, and memorable moments.

2. Authentic altruism does exist. People still do wonderful things without expecting anything in return because it is the right thing to do.

3. Accidental encounters can have positive, life-changing consequences only if you are open to learning from new experiences, even if those consequences don't sink in for years to come.

4. Don't throw your only set of keys high into the night sky.

Chapter 3
Grade School Switcheroo

From the age of eight till the age of 18, Zach and I spent most of our free time together. We were so set on hanging out that over the years we wore our parents down about it. Because of all the time spent in each other's company, the two of us became brothers, and we ended up spending most nights at each other's houses. From September to June, waking at 6:30 a.m., putting on our white polo shirts and navy-blue Dockers (a.k.a., Catholic school uniforms), playing a quick game of "Mike Tyson's Punch-Out," sometimes literally punching each other in the arm, and having breakfast, we were off to our respective schools.

Zach went to Cathedral, and I went to St. Mary's. Although Cathedral was actually closer to my parents' home, they had attended mass at St. Mary's, felt that it was a good fit, and had enrolled me when I was old enough to go to kindergarten. I had always enjoyed St. Mary's, but as Zach and I grew closer, we often talked about one of us switching schools so that we could spend even more time together. Zach always talked up Cathedral, and he was quick to point out that Cathedral was located closer to my parents' house and that

Cathedral's sports program was more successful than St. Mary's. The sports program detail was no small matter to me, as I (along with Zach) was passionate about baseball and basketball, and the two of us played catch, shot baskets, and battled each other in what thousands of games of one-on-one.

Nintendo became Super Nintendo, the Dyno Air BMX bike was introduced, slap bracelets came and went, everyone wanted to *Be Like Mike,* and Starter gear was all the rage by the time we hit seventh grade. It had taken years of coercion, but by this time Zach had eroded my indifference and persuaded me to talk to my parents about switching to Cathedral. To Zach, this task was the second Crusade, "Operation Crusader Conversion." To me, talking to my parents was just to kick the idea around and get their reaction, which was lukewarm at first.

My mom said, "I thought you loved St. Mary's. You've been there since kindergarten. All your classmates like you, and all the teachers know you. You only have one year left; why switch now?" To a reasonable 30-year-old recalling the situation, I have to admit that Mom was logical, sensible—and right. But it was too late: Zach's psychological guerilla warfare had taken hold. To a 13-year-old dreaming of the opportunity to spend *a whole school year* with his best friend, things like logic and common sense were meaningless. To adults, an conversation such as this is just a small occurrence in a day filled with far more important goals to accomplish. Commutes, meetings, and bills command their attention. During these seemingly mundane conversations the kid always has the advantage because kids have *time*. To them, these are the biggest considerations in their lives, and by the time I had turned 13 I knew that the only way to make things happen was to remain steadfast and determined. This discussion was not over, and I knew it was time to begin chipping away at my parents' resolve to keep me at St. Mary's.

Like Ralphie dropping hints about his desire for a Red Rider BB Gun in *A Christmas Story*, I was always trying to find a way to work Cathedral into my conversations with my parents. I repeated stories that Zach had told me and relayed points he had made about why Cathedral was the better school for me. At the advice of my strategist, I took the opportunity every morning to point out to my mother that if I went to Cathedral she wouldn't have to drive me to school since I could ride my bike. At one point it seemed to be working, but seventh grade was moving quickly, and I felt progress was too slow. I can remember one event in particular that convinced me I needed to shift "Operation Crusader Conversion" into overdrive.

Early in the seventh-grade boys' basketball season, Cathedral visited St. Mary's for our first matchup. In all our prior meetings dating back to fifth grade, we were never able to beat Cathedral, and they usually handled our team pretty easily. This was due to a manchild Crusader named Brian Amann, a shocking six feet tall at 11 years of age. At game's end, the Crusaders' final team score and Brian's personal tally were usually one and the same, and his extended family, which averaged 50 percent of the Cathedral crowd, let everyone in the gym know it.

Zach wasn't much of a scorer, but at point guard his own man-child totals—assists in his case—rivaled that of John Stockton dishing the rock to Karl Malone. Knowing that I'd be playing against Zach and Brian (who had also become a friend), I was pretty pumped up and wanted to impress everyone playing and watching. In all modesty, I carried the team on my back all season, and I knew if we had any chance of winning I'd have to be the man in charge on our end of the court. The game started off well. Utilizing my extra motivation, I took every opportunity to drive to the basket. Finding open lanes and hitting open shots, I was putting on the performance that I'd hoped for. By the time the buzzer sounded for halftime, our team was actually ahead, and I'd scored all but a handful of my team's points.

As the third quarter began, I was riding high, hoping to do whatever it took to maintain our lead and clinch a big victory against the Crusaders. Early on, however, it became clear to me that the second half would not go as well as the first. As I carried the ball over half court for the first play of the second half, my best friend greeted me in a tenacious defensive position. Zach had that look on his face, the look that gave me comfort when we were teammates playing other duos in two-on-two, the look that said, "I'm shutting you down." Cathedral had switched from a zone to a box and one, with the "one" trying his best to stop the other team's top player from scoring. Zach was a smothering defender and having played with (and against) me so often, he knew my game well—my strong hand, my driving tendencies, my best moves. He defended me tightly, leaving no room for comfort. He forced me to pass the ball rather than shoot, and St. Mary's quickly lost its lead and couldn't climb back.

Feeling down after the game, I was greeted warmly by Zach and his father, Don. My parents, the Cathedral coach, and some other people were still hanging around the gym.

"Good game," Zach said, with a smirk on his face.

"Good game," I replied. "Good defense second half."

"I told Tim I could guard you man to man," he said.

As we continued our conversation, Don and Tim (Zach's coach) were talking with my parents. We all hung out for a few more minutes, and Don mentioned a couple of times that I should switch schools so that I could see Zach more, adding that he thought I could start on a team that had a chance to win the Catholic Diocese championship. I don't know if it was because of the excitement of the evening, the bonding time my parents had with Don and Tim, or something else, but as we were driving home, my parents asked me if I were still interested in going to Cathedral. They were opening up to the idea, and after a few more conversations, I'd convinced them to let me make the move. I was headed to Cathedral for a year with my best friend!

Before I knew it, I was standing in front of the entire class during a visit that was part of the enrollment process toward the end of seventh grade. It was spring and the days were getting warmer, but most of the

Catholic schools in Belleville did not have air conditioning. The heat was on, literally and figuratively. Zach had quite a knack for talking up his friends, and he wasted no time doing just that while introducing me to the class. Standing in the limelight for the first time at Cathedral, I knew I'd have to fill some huge shoes, fashioned by the exaggerations of Zach and fed into the imaginations of the classmates I'd soon be attending class with every day. I learned about some of the things I'd have to live up to from the first thing out of many of my classmates' mouths.

"So how many kids did you beat in arm wrestling?"

"Did you really jump Richland creek on your Dyno Air?"

"I heard you're a computer hacker."

"Tell me about your family's weapons."

Like most gossip, all of these "embellishments" contained a grain of truth. I had beaten at least one other kid in arm wrestling. I had jumped a ramp that was right next to the creek. I was becoming familiar with Mom's new computer and the recently discovered "World Wide Web," and my Dad had bought me a .22-caliber rifle to learn how to shoot. I realized with Zach, though, that I'd have to be quite liberal in my assessment of reality when discussing every one of my so-called accomplishments. With the prospect of seeing my classmates daily, I knew I couldn't uphold a completely skewed version of reality long-term. I had to be vague on specifics, stay heavy on comedy and sarcasm, and dial things down over time until everyone came to know me for the person I really was. By employing that strategy—vagueness, comedy, and familiarity—I successfully managed their expectations. For the majority of that school year I enjoyed "new-kid-in-school" status: familiar enough that I was one of the guys, mysterious enough that the girls liked me.

Morals of the Story

1. To get what you want you can never give up.

2. Managing expectations is crucial to forming relationships, both personal and professional.

3. It's never too late to make a change.

4. Catapult your own success by relying on your immediate social network. In sports, the catapult might be the physical ability of a bearded 11-year-old.

Chapter 4
CAUGHT IN THE ACT

One of the exercises that Zach has his freshmen college students complete is called a "friend inventory." He asks students to describe the characteristics of their friends, rank-order these individuals from most important to least important, and think about the reasons that certain people make it to the upper echelons of friendship while other people remain at the acquaintance or hallway-head-nod level. Students always enjoy this activity because it forces them to think about friendship as a system of reciprocity from a rational- actor perspective. That is, by making lists of friends and desired characteristics, they begin to realize what they value in friendships and can contemplate how they act in relation to others. They also make pro-and-con lists for actions that move people up and down their friend hierarchy. The rational-actor approach to friendships allows students to see how and why they relate to specific people and teaches them about their friendship habits, quirks, and pet peeves. They can see exactly why they are best friends with someone or why they made the choice to de-friend someone in life (and on Facebook).

Without exception, every time Zach has students complete this activity, students mention that a defining characteristic of their closest friends is that they have gotten into and out of trouble with these individuals. They learn how their friends will respond in difficult situations and rank them accordingly. In essence, the students are talking about a test of loyalty without ever calling it that. It isn't necessarily just the act of causing trouble that forms a close bond between people but rather how each individual responds to the reality of getting caught. This is the real test of loyalty in a friendship. For Zach and me, ever since the night of the spontaneous search party, we realized that we loved to pull pranks and bend the rules. We've had plenty of opportunities to test our loyalty during our 23-year friendship. We were lucky enough to find ourselves in the center of many (naively well-intentioned) troublemaking activities that taught us how to properly frame our responses to authority figures, how to keep quiet when necessary, and how to support each other regardless of the consequences. The following three chapters do not recommend getting into trouble, breaking laws, or routinely disobeying authority figures, but they do encourage people to take risks, think about how they deal with unpleasant, unexpected situations, and possibly learn from how Zach and I dealt with our challenges.

Chapter 5
Extreme Truckers and Middle Fingers

When Zach and I were in grade school, rollerblading became the cool thing to do. Accordingly, we would throw on our blades and skate around the neighborhood and, once we were good enough, around the city of Belleville. We got to the point where we could do a variety of tricks like riding handrails, hopping trash cans, and jumping stairs. Pushing the limit was our unofficial motto. Zach and I often challenged each other to difficult skating tricks to see who would come out on top. Because our skill levels were pretty equal, most of the time we would meet each other's challenges. One of our favorite places to roller blade was in the parking lot of Roosevelt grade school, which was directly behind the street we lived on.

Roosevelt had a large, smooth blacktop parking lot that was ideal for roller blading. Not only that, but every other summer the school would resurface the lot, so we had a new surface at all times that was perfect for developing our speed-skating skills, for perfecting our skills skating backward, and for setting up obstacle courses with framed family photos, vinyl records, and other useless things (to kids) we found lying around our houses. The lot also had three or four landscaped medians that separated different parking areas, and these were good for speed skating around. One hot summer day we were going through our normal competitive routine, this time seeing who could complete the obstacle course more quickly, when Zach came up with one of his silly bets featuring yet another unexpected outcome.

Highway 15 was located at the top of a hill about a quarter mile south of Roosevelt's parking lot. This highway was a popular route for truckers to get to the larger interstates and was a shortcut between downtown St. Louis and southern Illinois. Not many of the non-truck-driving public used highway 15, however, because it went through East St. Louis, which is a dangerous area if you didn't know where you are going.

Zach must have been getting bored with our skating routine because he threw out the following bet: "Hey, Dave. I bet you a million dollars I can get a trucker to come chase us."

"You're insane!" I said. "No way." Then, an instant later, "You're on." We proceeded to shake hands, which, if you don't know, is the international symbol for a legitimate bet.

Be aware that Hwy. 15, in addition to being a quarter mile away from the lot, was some 30 to 40 feet higher in elevation, as well. The speed limit was 65 on that stretch of road, so Zach was going to have a scant few seconds to get the attention of a trucker, let alone get him to exit the highway a few miles down the road, drive back to where we were, and enter the Roosevelt parking lot. I thought this was going to be an easy win for me.

Zach took off for the east end of the parking lot and stopped. I wasn't sure what he was doing at first, but then it hit me. He was going to wait for a trucker to appear on the highway and would then skate in the same direction the driver was headed while simultaneously trying to get his attention. At first I thought Zach had roughly the length of a football field to do this, but I had forgot that Roosevelt had a second, equally large parking lot at the rear of the school, which Zach and I didn't skate on because the surface was usually covered with gravel. A large, rusty chain connected to two yellow concrete poles separated the two lots.

Once Zach spotted an 18-wheeler on 15, he took off as fast as he could and immediately started yelling and waving his two middle fingers in the direction of the truck. I laughed at how ridiculous this looked—what kind of crazy person would yell at someone inside the cab of a truck a quarter mile away, who is driving on a hill, and expect to get that person's attention? It would be like an ant trying to get the attention of an elephant. This thought apparently did not enter Zach's mind, as he was determined to get this trucker to notice him. He continued screaming and taunting the driver as they both picked up speed. "Get down here, man! Help me win a million dollars! I'll give you ten percent!" he screeched.

As Zach neared the second parking lot, hardly seeming to skip a beat or pay attention to the onrushing hazard, he soared over the rusty chain and landed confidently and comfortably on the lot's rough surface, in continuance of his zany pursuit. The lot wrapped around the school, so I lost sight of Zach for about 30 seconds. While I daydreamed about how I would spend my million dollars, Zach slowly came skating around the opposite side of the building on the sidewalk. He looked crushed.

Acknowledging his defeat, he said, "You can take this off the amount you already owe me from our basketball bets."

I agreed. This was a worthy bet to win because it involved such a crazy stunt and story that I could then retell to our mutual friends—and adding a bit of social humiliation to our bets was always fair game. I was all smiles at this point, and Zach was ready to go home until I convinced him to stay and do some fast figure eights with me for a few more minutes. As we began the third or fourth cycle of our eights, we heard it: the deep bellow of a truck engine. It cut through the air, hitting the pit of our stomachs instantly. I will never forget the sheer terror associated with that sound and the sight of that 18-wheeler roaring into the Roosevelt parking lot. The driver did not appear to be there for a nap. He was out for blood.

We were paralyzed at first—now we knew what a deer in a set of headlights feels like. The smiles dissolved. The bets disappeared. This was real—we were going to have to skate to save our lives. We believed that this man literally wanted to run us down in broad daylight in Belleville, Illinois. Zach's insults and actions had pushed this guy to the edge of some psychological abyss, and he was looking for company on the trip down. He would not stop until we covered his tires. I felt a thousand different emotions pour into my brain and body: anger, confusion, surprise, disgust, fear, awe—and remorse.

Zach's big mouth and inappropriate gesturing had done us in. My life not only flashed before my eyes, I envisioned my epitaph: "Here lies David Ponder. He was run over by a truck because he made a stupid bet." What about my grieving parents? And who would feed the dog? Would the guy get caught or would he get away with it? And how the hell did he see Zach from that damn highway? Questions raced through my mind as I tried to figure out on the fly how to get away from this homicidal maniac. I thought he must have had the eyes of a hawk, the kind of hawk that glides 200 feet in the air and spots a mouse grazing in a field. He also must have had a bad … life.

My legs felt glued to the blacktop, but before I knew it, they were pumping, and I was skating as fast as I had ever skated. Zach and I both headed for the area of the parking lot that had the landscaped medians. Unless the truck was going to jump the medians, which it could have, this might give us just enough time to get into the street and back to my house. The driver gunned it and shot into the parking lot at what seemed like a hundred miles an hour but was probably closer to seven. He headed straight for Zach and me until we raced toward the medians, when, instead of slowing down and making a sharp turn to follow us, he jerked the wheel in our direction and darn near jack-knifed his entire rig. He was one angry mother-trucker.

The medians gave us just enough time to get to the street. I thought Zach and I had talked through our escape plan, but that must have been wishful thinking, because at the last moment Zach went up the alley, and I shot down the street to the empty lot directly behind my house and garage. Once there, I knew I could sneak through the breezeway behind the garage and make it safely into my backyard. I would be safe because my mom was home, and she would call the police (this was pre-cell-phone America). Unfortunately for Zach, the alley that he had ducked into was located directly across from the Roosevelt parking lot entrance, so the truck driver was able to continue his pursuit. Fearing the worst, I turned my head to get a view of what was going on, and saw that the truck had barreled into the alley.

"Oh, God, he's killed Zach," I thought. By this time, still moving at full speed, I turned to see the truck try to back out of the alley and head in my direction. With my huge head start, I skated off the road and ran up the grassy hill where, upon entering my backyard, I could've slowed down, but after the *Maximum Overdrive* massacre of my best friend I was taking no chances. What I didn't realize till later was that the alley had been too narrow for the truck and that the driver was struggling to back the rig out of its tight position. As the front of the truck began to show, I prayed that Zach's body would not be smeared across the grill. It wasn't! It turned out he had escaped and made it to the other

Friendship, LLC

end of the alley—South 5th Street, the street we lived on. I ran through the breezeway and greeted Zach, who was skating down my driveway in tears. We ran into the house and proceeded to tell my mom what had happened, leaving out some of the key parts such as Zach's middle fingers, the taunting, and the bet. By the time she walked out of the house to investigate, the mysterious trucker had disappeared. To this day, few people believe the story of our near-death experience.

Morals of the Story

1. You don't need to impress the people who are closest to you because they already love you.

2. True friends stick together regardless of the consequences.

3. Obscene gestures can awaken homicidal tendencies in sleep-deprived truckers.

4. Rollerblades don't make good getaway vehicles.

Chapter 6
Antenna Removal Service

South 5th Street on the west side of Belleville was an exciting neighborhood to grow up in. There were plenty of grade school guys to run around with, a few grade school girls who were good enough athletes to play with the boys and good looking enough to keep us on our toes, and a handful of high school guys that we all admired. What was even better was that our parents all knew each other and got along. My Dad and Dave's parents knew some of the high school guys pretty well, and they expected those guys to watch out for us, which they did. They took Dave and me under their wing and taught us about all sorts of important things: how to kiss a girl, how to blow things up, how to smoke a cigarette, and how to play the drums, all things that any responsible parent would want their seventh-grade boys to know. As we got older, they took us to concerts, let us come to their parties, and gave us free reign to hang out in their garages and basements, even if they weren't home.

That said, in the interest of fairness and saving people's reputations, Dave and I feel compelled to point out that our high school friends were considered anything but dorky for hanging out with seventh graders, and in fact, were standout athletes, aspiring musicians, and some of the most popular kids in their schools. They always had good-looking girls coming over, and they drank beer and smoked cigarettes (and other things) on a regular basis. They allowed us to hang out because we weren't "normal" seventh graders. We brought some talent to the table. Let me tell you what I mean.

It was at this point that Dave was really developing his computer-literacy skills. My Mom, Maureen, had purchased the first computer that Apple had produced, the Apple I introduced in 1976, and she quickly became a computer expert. She could already type faster than lightning due to her astute court reporting skills, and now she could understand how and why computers worked, just as the Internet was gaining momentum. Dave's Dad knew about my Mom's computer abilities and would always ask her about the hottest computers on the market. Art ended up buying the best computer money could buy—a pattern throughout our lives—and he encouraged Dave to learn as much as he could about them. Dave's newly purchased super-computer, combined with the knowledge and tutelage of my Mom and a friend named Hector, helped Dave become the technology guru he is today. But even in fifth grade, Dave had a commanding knowledge of how to troubleshoot computer problems. The high school guys knew this, and his willingness to help them with their computers made him a valuable friend.

Friendship, LLC

If Dave was 9 out of 10 on the computer literacy scale, I was a 5. It wasn't my knowledge of DOS, Microsoft Word, or my ability to clear the cache on Internet Explorer that made me a desirable companion to the high school crowd. It was my smart mouth, my sarcasm, and my evasiveness.

I always had (and still have) what most people would call a "foul mouth." Even at a young age, I found it funny that you shouldn't say certain words, because I understood that meanings change over time. (I'm aware that language is arbitrary and conventional, but that's a conversation for another day.) One outcome of my "defensive dominance" personality was that I could (and can) spout four-letter words so stylishly that some might call it art. My wife, Kizzy, has already agreed that my epitaph will read: *Here lies Zach Schaefer. He struggled to be pleasant. He tried to be useful. He loved to cuss.* Sizing people up and being able to come back with a zinger that embarrassed an adversary brought me joy, even if it was a defensive mechanism tied to other psychological issues. I took this skill as a point of pride … and so did the high school guys.

When our buddies threw parties, many of their friends would wonder why two grade schoolers were hanging out. Such conversations usually ended like this:

Friend X: Who are these kids?

Brandon/Damian/John (our buddies): They're our friends.

Friend X: That was nice of their mommy and daddy to let them out to play.

Zach: That was nice of your parents to keep you around even though you were an accident.

[Lots of laughing.]

Friend X: You have a big mouth for such a little guy.

Zach: You're very observant.

Friend X: Keep running your mouth, and I'll shut it for you.

Zach: You gonna bark all day, little doggie, or are you gonna bite? (as I prepare for the foot chase)

Friend X (leaping from his chair, usually knocking over drinks and ash trays): You're dead.

Zach: If you can catch me. (I run up the stairs and into the yard, where I out run the friend as he chases me around the neighborhood, not giving up the taunting during the pursuit. The friend eventually keels over in exhaustion.).

The best part about all this was that once my buddies' friends witnessed my sarcastic mouth, they liked me for it, even the ones who chased me. Over time, Dave and I took on a semi-celebrity status at these neighborhood gatherings, saying certain unmentionable things to people our friends didn't like while the rest of the partygoers would watch the outcasts chase us around the yard. It was a game we never lost, meaning we never got caught. As you can see, we had an interesting relationship with our neighborhood elders, one that involved an element of mutual respect.

Dave and I were always looking for new ways to impress our friends, and one Saturday afternoon Dave came up with a brilliant idea that he outlined to me and a few guys from the neighborhood. Dave said we should tie a string across West Cleveland, a busy street perpendicular to South 5th, just high enough to hit car antennas and make them slap against the cars. This would startle the drivers, and we would get a good laugh out of it. We scouted around our basements and attics until we found some old kite string. Because Dave and I weren't tall enough, we asked one of our high school friends, Damian, to tie the string on each side of the street for us.

Damian waited for a lull in traffic and then tied the string to a No Parking sign on the east side of the street; once the coast was clear, he sprinted across the street and tied the other end to a *Slow Children* sign. He completed his task perfectly, as the string seemed to be the ideal height to hammer the antenna and send it snapping against the roof of a car. We ducked behind an old Dodge Ram pickup parked on West Cleveland and waited for our first victim. Within minutes a man driving a silver Honda Accord appeared at the top of the hill. Our hearts began to pound, we started sweating and smiling, and our hands got clammy. We had no idea what to expect.

As the man approached our tripwire, we saw there was a woman in the passenger seat. The man obviously did not see the string and was falling for our prank; what an idiot. When his car, which was traveling a leisurely 30 miles per hour or so, hit the string, his antenna became ensnared but held strong. It was a battle of kite string versus antenna. Kite string won. The man drove about 15 feet past the signs before his antenna ripped clear off the car. This, unfortunately, wasn't in our plan.

The next few seconds involved two equally scary sounds: a car screeching to a halt and the pitter-patter of my friends running away from the scene of the crime. I was the closest to the car when it stopped, and I was panic stricken that the driver had seen me. At that point I mentally added another category to the theory that explains how people deal with unexpected threats: fight or flight. Instead of running or fighting, I stood frozen with *fear*. I was utterly petrified and saw myself locked in a jail cell with an ax-murderer. What was even scarier was the thought of calling my Mom to bail me out. Yikes. How did a plan that seemed so right go so wrong? The driver got out of his car and began to notify me, in a not-so-polite tone of voice, that our actions could have killed someone. I wish I knew what the phrase *melodramatic hyperbole* meant back then, because I could have let this guy know that was what he was using. He went on to suggest he was going to call my parents and the police. *Yada-yada-yada*.

To rub salt into the wound, after slowly creeping up the street and trying to hold myself together, I walked into my house to see my friends, brother, and father sitting around the TV watching standup comedy and eating a Pizza Hut meat-lover's pizza. Sobbing like a baby, I exploded and let them all have it, including Dad—who at that point had no knowledge of the antenna experiment. Having been lectured for the past few minutes by the irate driver, I wanted to have my friends explain why they bolted and left me for dead.

Friendship, LLC

I discovered that they thought I'd run in the opposite direction, and they weren't worried because I was the fastest runner in the group. They didn't know that my emotional molasses had kept me planted on West Cleveland. As soon as Dave learned what had happened, he immediately apologized and asked for forgiveness. After we explained the whole story to my Dad, he left to see if the driver was still around to offer to pay for his damaged car. We eventually started laughing at the idea of this guy having to explain to his buddies how a tiny 12-year-old had removed his antenna free of charge and then withstood a 10-minute dressing down, without giving his name or the names of his fellow saboteurs or even so much as shedding a tear in front of him. All I kept saying to the gentlemen was that "it wasn't supposed to rip it off" and that I was "very sorry." The tears didn't flow until I saw my friends—and they were tears of guilt, fear, and anger. As we finished our pizza, Dave was the only person who offered an apology and asked for forgiveness. What a guy, what a friend.

Morals of the Story

1. It takes a real man to ask for forgiveness, even if the "man" is only 12.

2. Asking and granting forgiveness is the lifeblood of lasting relationships.

3. If you are raising hell and the other hell-raisers run, don't wait around to see what happens.

4. Pizza always tastes better after escaping trouble.

Chapter 7
Prank Calls and Police

One of our favorite ways to kill time in grade school and high school was to make prank phone calls. Zach and I got hold of an old Jerky Boys CD and an *Eddie Murphy Raw* video that we would listen to and watch for hours. The Jerky Boys taught us to push limits when it came to "acceptable forms of humor," and *Eddie Murphy* taught us the importance of effective delivery, timing, and the shock-and-awe of offensive words. We even put a few of the Jerky Boys' greetings on our parents' answering machines. One of the funnier ones was that of an evil voice cackling over a roar of electrical popping, saying that if the caller did not leave a message, an innocent kitty would be electrocuted. Not the most tasteful thing to do but funny nonetheless. But Zach and I being Zach and I, we couldn't just pull pranks, tell stories about them, and be done with it. No. We had to make a *competition* out of it. So we created a few standards by which we could "judge" the effectiveness of our adventures.

For one, we would time our calls to see how long we could keep the other party on the line. We would ratchet up the outrageousness of the content being discussed, starting with the mundane, such as offering phony telemarketing products and services and harassing restaurant managers with fake food-poisoning claims, to more provocative subjects, such as answering adult classified ads and ordering props for pornographic movies. One time, posing as movie producers, we phoned a company called Midwest Petroleum, a local energy outfit, and asked for 50-gallon drums of lubricating jelly for an orgy scene. Another time, we called a retail store with the self-imposed requirement that we could only say two words: "butt plugs."

The biggest challenge was to see who could keep the victim on the phone for the longest time without breaking character or laughing. Holding in our laughter was difficult because we often performed our pranks for an audience of as many as 10 friends. But after several years of making these calls, Zach and I had become masters at staying in character and delivering sober conversations. Our friends were amazed … especially when we invited them to participate and they couldn't last 10 seconds.

There was also a method to our madness. We always dialed *67 before we called, to block our number from showing up on caller IDs and to keep our calls from being traced. Also, we made all our calls on speaker phone, adding to the challenge of keeping a straight face in front of our friends. Another approach we took to enliven things was to arbitrarily open the phone book and start dialing numbers until we got an answer. To our delight, we usually "went live" within two or three calls. Before describing our encounter with the local law-enforcement, I want to describe three brief pranks that will give you a better idea of our abilities.

$1,000,000 Winner

"Ma'am, you have just won ONE MILLION DOLLARS! How do you feel?" Repeating this phrase as many times as possible in my best game-show-host voice was the sole purpose of yet another prank call. I had called one or two people who quickly hung up on me before I reached someone who sounded like, well, my grandmother. Our victim had a soft, sweet voice and must have been lonely, because I was able to repeat this phrase some 15 times before being overcome with laughter and having to end the call. The poor woman kept saying that she did not register for contests, and I assured her that had we pulled her information from DMV records, but more important, that she was the winner of "ONE MILLION DOLLARS!" She may have had a touch of dementia, because she kept redirecting the conversation to her small dogs, which I could hear barking in the background. Before I broke up in laughter, I told her that she "could buy new dogs, even start an entire dog farm, because she had just won ONE MILLION DOLLARS!"

Hardees's Family Reunion

I came up with the idea of calling a fast-food restaurant and asking if I could rent out the facility to host a family reunion. Zach and I decided on a nearby Hardee's because we liked their fried chicken and knew some of the employees. Knowing that fried chicken was a southern favorite, I decided to use my best Colonel Sanders/Foghorn Leghorn impression. My aim was to convince the manager to close the restaurant to the public in order to accommodate our party, which consisted of 150 people. At first the manager was uncooperative, saying that that many partygoers would violate corporate and city policies, to say nothing of fire codes regarding maximum capacity. More important, there was simply no way that that many people could fit into the restaurant. I then asked if their policies were set in stone. I went on to guarantee that our family would buy 400 buckets of chicken, and if the customer capacity was reached, that the manager could open the roof to accommodate the rest of our guests. To Zach's astonishment, I kept the manager on the phone for nearly 10 minutes, time which included a conference call to corporate headquarters to discuss policy exceptions and roof access. I was so successful with the call that by the time I ended it my Catholic guilt had kicked in, and I explained what I was doing and apologized. I told the manager that I would call the corporate office and fess up to his bosses if he felt I'd put his job in jeopardy. He actually laughed and said it wasn't a problem and that business was pretty slow during the call. If nothing else, we gave him a good story to share with his employees.

Cracker Barrel Food Poisoning

As you know by now, I wasn't the only skilled 5th Street prankster. Zach was quite good, too. I was better at keeping people on the line and suppressing laughter while Zach excelled with wacky voices, celebrity impressions, and making sound effects. One of Zach's best pranks was convincing a manager at a local Cracker Barrel that Zach's entire family had gotten food poisoning from the restaurant's biscuits and gravy. One of our closest friends, Justin, was present for this prank call session. He appreciated the inherent competition and the level of difficulty of prank calling, and he was present for many of our calls. In this particular call, Zach's voice resembled Al Bundy's from *Married with Children*, and he continually screamed "off phone," yelling to his "wife" (me, who was making loud vomiting sounds) that he was taking care of the situation and assuring his kids that they would get better. The background-yelling technique was vintage Jerky Boys. With Cracker Barrel, Zach went into graphic details of what his "family" was experiencing and described the exact time, table, order, and server associated with the family's dining debacle. Zach was trying to get the manager to send him $50 worth of gift certificates, and he seemed to be about to pull it off. But Zach knew he couldn't give out his real address, so he made one up. At that point, the manager asked Zach to pick the certificates up in person, once his family's illness had subsided, so that he could personally apologize for the incident, a request to which Zach replied, "If you don't want your country store covered in vomit and don't want to hear from my attorney, I suggest you mail them."

It turned out the manager wasn't the type who responded well to threats. He said, "Look, friend. I'm sorry for your experience, but you either pick these up in person or you can forget about them."

"No, you look," Zach said without hesitation. "I can find out where you live. If you don't want envelopes of vomit Fed-Exed to your house every day for the next two weeks, I suggest you send me those certificates."

This one-upmanship continued for another few minutes until Zach and the manager were screaming obscenities at one another. Zach ended the call by saying, "I hope you've enjoyed wasting twenty minutes of your time being pranked by a 13-year-old. Explain that to your wife and boss. Later." What made this call even funnier was the image of the manager freaking out, cussing, and pacing around the restaurant. Not the most moral thing to do to someone, but it was damn funny. Karma always catches up, however.

Ratcheting it Up: Panorama Bowling Lanes

We were now prank call masters. Our friends and schoolmates had heard of our exploits and would feed us new ideas to use on unsuspecting victims. These were always fun, but we needed a way to step up our game .... on our own terms. We were brainstorming ideas one afternoon during rounds of Mortal Kombat at a local bowling alley called Panorama Lanes. We spent a lot of time at Panorama because it was within walking distance of our homes. It just so happened that I knew the guy working behind the counter this particular afternoon—we had attended St. Mary's grade school together. He was a few years older than I and probably didn't remember me very well, but I remembered him. From what I recalled around the halls and playgrounds of St. Mary's, "Bryan Smith" was nice, quiet, and shy. And then it hit me: we can prank Bryan while he's at work.

I ran my idea by Zach and he agreed. This would up the ante and allow us to add new elements to our pranks to make them even more realistic and funny. The beauty of this prank was that we used the pay phone *inside* the bowling alley to pull it off. We would be far enough away that Bryan couldn't hear us but close enough that we could see his actions in real time. I placed the calls.

"Panorama Lanes. How can I help you," he said.

"Hi, Smitty. I can see you," I said.

"Excuse me," he replied.

"You're not safe, Smitty. See those guys at the NBA Jam arcade? The one wearing the Metallica shirt isn't happy with you. He knows what you did to his sister."

Of course, I was ad-libbing at this point. I didn't know the guy with the Metallica shirt, and I was pretty certain that if he did have a sister, Bryan probably had never even met her. But with that statement we could see that we got Bryan thinking. The gears in his head were grinding away, searching for a recollection of any action he'd recently directed toward any woman that could be remotely construed as offensive. We had struck a nerve, we saw the weakness in Smitty's eyes, and like lions, we pounced. This is the part of the prank, any good prank, where you turn up the heat. You crank that knob till it won't crank no more, and then, if you really want a good story, you break it off. By now, Zach had become the information gatherer. Pretending to be playing the Street Fighter arcade next to the Metallica shirted customer, he was on reconnaissance, spying on the conversation Metallica was having while at the same time keeping tabs on Bryan's body language. He would return to let me know the most recent occurrences, which I could exploit on my next call. For example, knowing that the guy was going to get a pizza at the snack bar, as he'd just mentioned to his friend, allowed us to turn his behavior, completely unrelated to Bryan Smith, into a sinister ritual of preparation for the attack he would soon perpetrate.

"He's going to get pizza, Smitty. That's the sign. He told his friends to meet up at the snack bar when he was eating pizza. They're gonna jump you."

Taking a break from bowling and video games, the snack bar was packed with high school-aged kids looking to kill time on a 90-plus-degree day in beautiful Belleville, Illinois. On that day, though, to Bryan Smith, they were an angry mob fueling up for the attack. Zach and I then carried out our ultimate move, the cherry on top of the prank-call sundae. Without recognizing we were crossing the line from prank to death threat, we placed a handwritten note under a newspaper on the newspaper rack that simply read, "You're dead, Smitty."

We now made our last call to tell him where to find the message. We knew this had escalated into something we didn't want to be around for, so we walked back to Zach's house, stroking our egos and rehashing our mastery of the prank trade. Within the hour, Zach's Dad offered to drive us to Blockbuster Video to rent movies. Don rented three to five movies at a time, alphabetically. That night, he got *Beverly Hills Cop*, *Big Trouble in Little China,* and *Brian's Song,* since he had recently looped back to the beginning of the alphabet, and he was in the B's. Speaking of the letter "B," Blockbuster is now bankrupt.

It was as we passed the bowling alley on our way to Blockbuster that we saw the red, white, and blue lights dancing off the treetops. Zach and I looked at each other and thought, "My God, what did we do?"

Three police cars blocked the entrance to the bowling alley and another one was pulled directly in front of the main entrance. There were 30-40 people milling about the parking lot, including Bryan, and he was talking to the police. We knew we were toast. As our conversation became more anxious, matching the nervous nonverbals on our faces, Don realized that we had done something wrong. Instead of ensnaring ourselves in a web of lies, we decided to tell him the whole story. He did NOT find it funny but did add an unexpected twist.

"Did you physically hurt anyone or steal or vandalize anything?" he asked. Adamantly shaking hour heads, we said that we had not done any such things.

"Then you are to never speak a word of this to anyone unless you want to go to prison for a felony. You are wasting my tax dollars and the police's time. What if something serious happened on the other side of town and these officers could not respond in time because of your stupid prank? Let this be a lesson to you. I'd better not hear of you doing any more b.s. that gets the police involved."

As our stomachs continued to shrink and our voices continued to quiver, we were relieved that we weren't headed to jail. Zach's Dad had our backs but also clearly showed us the negative consequences of having too much fun and going too far.

Morals of the Story

1. Imagination and spontaneity are the spice of life.

2. A collaborative form of competition can help people achieve positive, unexpected results.

3. Having fun at another's expense is no fun at all.

4. If you want to make prank calls, stick to the phone lines and stay out of bowling alleys.

Chapter 8
THINKING BIG

During his doctoral studies, Zach and a few colleagues listened to an academic deliver a keynote address on how parents, teachers, and other role models should help young people (i.e., children and students) set realistic goals. The scholar said that mentors should encourage their mentees to develop career goals that are likely to be achieved, such as becoming a teacher, doctor, or lawyer, and to dissuade them from pursuing goals that are most likely unattainable, such as becoming a professional athlete, musician, or actor. Zach and his fellow graduate students debated the pros and cons of the presentation, and later he and I discussed the same point. At first, we both agreed with almost everything the academic had said (which also included a discussion of how an educated person has more developed social networks and more opportunities for financial and personal success than an under educated person). Then it hit us. We remembered that our childhood dream was to play in the National Basketball Association (NBA).

Literally every warm-weather day, at the end of our organized sports practices, Zach and I would spend hours playing basketball in my backyard. We truly believed we could both make it to the NBA, or at least get a scholarship to play basketball in college and go to school free of charge. The best part of this dream was that our parents encouraged us to pursue it. I specifically remember our fathers telling us that "anything is possible if you put your mind to it." (Note: They didn't mention that short white guys rarely make it in pro ball, no matter how good they are, but that's beside the point. In fact, I can clearly remember telling Zach's Dad, Don, that I thought I'd have a legitimate chance if I grew to be 6'3", to which he replied, without a trace of irony, "Six-five would be better.")

Our parents fed our vision and helped us develop a plan for how we could become NBA superstars. The first step in that plan consisted of hours and hours and hours of practice. Next, we studied the game like professionals by analyzing basketball video tapes, watching televised games, and attending as many games in person as was humanly possible. Third, we went to every basketball camp that Belleville had to offer (and that our families could afford) and did whatever it took to get ourselves prepared to play high school ball. To work on his dribbling skills and get a feel for the ball, Zach took a basketball with him everywhere he went (including church). We idolized "Pistol" Pete Maravich and picked up his moves from a film we had watched about him. We knew what we had to do to make it to the NBA, and we were well on our way, or so we thought. Then reality smacked us in the face: we were short and skinny and those two qualities don't make good NBA players, let alone high school players.

Friendship, LLC

My point is this: why should Zach and I expect other young people to lower their aspirations and to limit their dreams, when we didn't do that ourselves? That would be hypocritical. You shouldn't place a ceiling on dreams. Should we tell kids to dream big, but not too big? That they can be whatever they want to be, as long as it statistically conforms to societal norms? What if some teacher had talked Steve Jobs into staying in college rather than changing the way humans communicate and use technology? What if Michael Jordan's coach had suggested he play another sport, baseball, perhaps? What if Albert Einstein's teacher had got upset for his argumentative nature and told him to pursue non-scientific endeavors? Many athletic, scientific, and artistic breakthroughs would not have occurred if people had listened to "advice" from trusted friends, teachers, colleagues, and parents. Zach and I were lucky that our parents had always supported us from an early age.

Our parents and siblings taught us that to have a positive impact in this world you need to change yourself, and to do that you need to change your environment and habits. The stories in the next three chapters detail the ways that Zach and I learned to hold high expectations for ourselves but also to manage those expectations based on societal norms. We learned to mix fantasy and reality, to take what life gave us and make the best of it, and to create a sense of self-confidence in everything we did (and do). In the end, we encourage kids (and adults) to dream big, because if nothing else you can make a positive impact while following your dreams and learn something about yourself—like going *beyond* the limits placed on you by others.

Chapter 9
Hustling Our Way to the NBA

"I'll bet you a million bucks I can hit this shot!" This bet was made daily at the Ponder house during games of H-O-R-S-E, as Dave and I spent countless hours sharpening our basketball skills and planting the seeds of our dream to make it to the NBA. We'll never forget the day that Art, Dave's Dad, put in an adjustable basketball hoop, which offered a huge advantage because it meant we could lower the rim to practice our dunks. What grade school kids wouldn't want to learn how to dunk? Well played Art!

It was a muggy Saturday morning. I had spent the night at Dave's, and we woke up to the feast that Mary, Dave's Mom, always prepared: scrambled eggs with cheese, jellied toast, biscuits and gravy, hash browns, ham, bacon, orange juice, coffee and milk … heaven for two sets of growing brothers. As Dave and I finished our meals and leapt from the table to begin our daily mischief making, Art asked us to meet him in the back for some yard work. We weren't happy, and for a split second I thought about heading back to my Dad's and leaving Dave to do the work alone, but I decided against that. After all, Dave would have stayed to help me.

In the backyard, we discovered shovels, a bag of cement, and a new basketball hoop still in its box. Seeing this, Dave and I couldn't have been more excited, and we immediately started dancing and jumping with joy. Dave had been begging Art to put in a hoop for years, and finally Art had relented, wisely enlisting the help of some *un*skilled laborers to get the hoop in the ground. At the time, we had no way of knowing that this basketball court would become a sanctuary for us, a safe environment that let us cut loose close to home, make new friends and meet new neighbors, practice our favorite sport—and have tons of fun while doing it.

Dreaming with Courage

The O'Fallon Ballpark was a large, white sheet-metal building that looked like a storage facility from the outside. The inside, however, was a magical sporting environment filled with soccer fields, a basketball court with an adjustable hoop, an arcade-game area, a snack bar that played pro games on TVs, and a gift shop. Five days a week this building was transformed from an empty metal vessel into a vibrant organism humming with energy. The building came alive as hundreds of sweaty kids in shin guards played in indoor soccer leagues as their corn-dog-eating parents devotedly watched and cheered them to victory. Happily, Dave and I were on the same team, which was always the best in our league. Dave was the goalie and I was the sweeper, which is the last line of defense before the goalie, and we were both voted to the all-star team several years in a row. While soccer was king at the Ballpark, there was a bonus: playing pick-up basketball games after our soccer matches were over. That's when we first got to exhibit our basketball skills in public.

Dave and I were all about strategy in the way we approached these games. If a game was in progress, someone on the sidelines would say, "We got next," which signaled that our team would play the winners of the current game. Since Dave and I wanted to play 2-on-2 games, if the previous game had more players we needed to figure out a way to get the winning team to drop down to two. So Dave came up with the idea that we would play their best two players for "rights" to the court. This was nothing less than genius, because the other kids didn't know that Dave and I had spent all those hours playing 1-on-1 and 2-on-2 at his home hoop.

Pick-up basketball was our favorite type of basketball, and our favorite sporting activity in general. Better yet, I was short and skinny and definitely did not look like a very good player. That's where our opponents were always wrong. I used my quickness and ball-handling skills to go the hoop for fancy reverse layups, dunks, or kick-out passes to Dave for his deadly jump shot. We were virtually unstoppable on the Ballpark court, and we would literally have 20-30 people watching us play, kids and parents alike. Not only did we rarely lose a game, we displayed flair and confidence, some might even say cockiness. We would talk "clean trash," since there were parents and kids present, and we could easily burrow into our opponents' heads to get them off their game. In fact, we won most games before they began just by talking trash while shooting around.

Whenever our opponents thought they were really good or got too physical with us, since many of them were a year or two older and physically bigger and stronger, I would say, "Put your money where your mouth is. Play me one on one." Although I know exactly where I learned this phrase (the O'Fallon Park basketball courts), I'm not sure what gave me the courage to say it to older players, especially with so many spectators on edge during such tense moments, but I did. I suppose the competition fueled my intense desire to win and to prove that a short, skinny guy could still be a great player. On those occasions when someone would agree to play me for money, we would each approach our parents for $5-10, depending on the bet, and then let one of our friends hold the money during the game. I would usually say, "Make it, take it, play to 15, win by 2, play by 1s and 2s." This meant that each time I scored a basket I got the ball back, I had to win by at least 2 points, and each basket counted as 1 point, or 2 points if you were behind a certain line. Not only did I never lose a 1-on-1 game and Dave and I never lose a 2-on-2 game at the Ballpark, people rarely scored more than 4 or 5 points on us.

The best part about this whole experience was that parents would come up to us after the games to meet us and find out where we went to school. They would ask us about our coaches, what basketball camps we attended, and whether we played on traveling teams. As our proud parents watched us beat the older kids, the defeated players' parents would be chatting with our parents, complementing us on our play and asking how we played so well together. My parents told them that we played basketball four to five hours every weekday, probably eight to 10 hours on weekends, and spent a lot of time playing pick-up games at O'Fallon Park. People didn't quite know what to make of this, because the typical players who played in O'Fallon were mostly black teens or men who were in high school or who had played at nearby junior colleges.

The level of play and the intensity of these games were extremely high—very few white guys played and definitely no young, skinny white guys. You couldn't just say "I got next" on that court, because the regular players had to know you before they would let you play. My Dad always said that if you want to be the best you need to play the best, and he felt that it would help our game if we played against the guys at the park. The first time we went to the park, Dave and I were probably 12 years old and half the size of most of the other players. We just watched them play on a few different occasions, and then finally one of the friendlier players asked us to join in. They put us on separate teams so that we could guard each other and they could gauge our games. Needless to say, they were impressed. We became the unofficial mascots at the park, and as soon as we would get there we were immediately picked for every game. Eventually, the guys had us guard older players rather than each other. We had gained their trust and respect, because moving forward, anytime one of the guys would get too physical with us or would get upset that we were being allowed to play, five other guys would have our backs and get the naysayer to shut his mouth. These games taught us how to play physically, talk trash, value trust and respect, and on a deeper level, appreciate how sports can bring people from different backgrounds together to share and enjoy the same activities. The men overlooked real differences in age, race, lifestyle, and size—we all enjoyed the game together.

Dave and I heard about their basketball and life-lesson success stories and their failures, and they wanted us to learn from their mistakes. We loved our time in the park, and in the summers before and after eighth grade, we spent several days a week learning how to hustle and how to have confidence in our game. We'll never forget when one of our biggest supporters at the park turned to an overly aggressive player who was talking trash to him. "Put your money where your mouth is," he barked. As the words rolled off his tongue, Dave and I immediately smiled at each other. We now had some new trash to talk.

Art didn't realize that giving us that backyard hoop would have such a profound effect on who we would become and how we would develop as young men. Although we never made it to the NBA, we did win a couple hundred dollars hustling over the years. We also developed many wonderful friendships that helped us become better people.

Morals of the Story

Friendship, LLC

1. Don't let people with small dreams distract you from your big dreams.

2. To be the best in a profession or sport, you need to compete with and compare yourself to the best.

3. Focusing on similarities and overlooking differences leads to unexpected friendships and knowledge.

4. Always carry some cash in case you need to make and win an easy bet.

Chapter 10
Magical Bartenders

"What are those kids doing behind that bar? They aren't 21. Are they serving alcohol?" Don Schaefer spent more time around St. Peter's Cathedral church, school, and gymnasium than the priests, teachers, and coaches combined. He was a Eucharistic minister, a minister of hospitality, a greeter, a lector, and an instructor for the Rite of Christian Initiation for Adults. He organized breakfasts for homeless people every Saturday morning and cleaned the McCormack Center, the school gymnasium and theatre. Because Don had access to the center, we were also able to use the gym for basketball practice, and because the parish allowed us to use the gym, Don felt responsible to make sure it was always organized and clean. He extended his free cleaning services to other events at McCormack and would set up, tear down, and clean up events like wedding receptions, silent auctions, and dances. This was not a small facility—a typical wedding reception would often include more than 300 people. In addition to setting up hundreds of tables and chairs for each event, Don would also tear them down, put them on storage carts, mop up the entire gym, and clean up the bathrooms … all while tending bar during the actual events. Doing all of this saved the parish thousands of dollars because it didn't have to hire cleaning crews or bartenders. But this was a lot of work for one man, even Don Schaefer.

By the time Zach and I were in the seventh grade, Don would enlist our help to set up and tear down for these events. He would pay us with trips to our favorite restaurants, the movies, and the batting cages. When he bartended, he usually had another adult there to help him keep an eye on the event and clean up spills while he poured the drinks. One night his assistant wasn't able to help during a wedding reception, so Don asked us if we would be able to fill in. Obviously, he didn't want us serving alcohol or replacing kegs when they ran dry, but we could mop up spilled beer on the dance floor, restock soda, and make sure he had everything he needed. We agreed to help because he promised us a trip to Six Flags as a reward. We had no clue how much fun we would have that night and how much we would learn about the effects of alcohol on decision making.

At the time of this particular reception, Zach and I were really into magic tricks. My parents had taken us to a costume and magic shop in downtown St. Louis called Gibbol's. It was here that we first learned about the mystery and appeal of magic. One of the employees showed us several card and coin tricks. We were mesmerized, and my parents were out about $100 for purchasing two magic "starter kits." Zach and I ripped open the kits on the ride home and soon began practicing magic as often as we could, that is, when we weren't hustling kids on the basketball court, running around the neighborhood, or engaging in hijinks of one kind or another. I can't imagine how annoying all this magic must have been to our parents, siblings and friends, since they knew how all our tricks ended because we had practiced them over and over until we had mastered them.

Among our many tricks, our best involved a silver dollar and a quarter and was called Scotch and Soda. The magician used sleight of hand to deceive the audience into thinking that the quarter had disappeared, when in reality it had been "absorbed" into the silver dollar, which was a trick coin. Although our performances were usually one-man shows, Zach and I were able to feed off each other and turn a few simple tricks into more of a two-man presentation, a poor-man's Penn and Teller (minus the Libertarian politics and dry humor). We would make fun bets with our audience during the show and use our "innocent demeanor" to persuade people to participate. Because we were so confident in our skills, we would take our trick coins everywhere and put on impromptu performances even without being invited.

Once we agreed to help Don with the wedding reception, Zach asked him if we could do some tricks while the guests were waiting in line for beer, and he let us. Our first few stunts turned some smiles and got us pats on the back, but that was not quite the response we were looking for, which was money. The people would smile and say, "Got some cute kids there."

"Cute? *Cute?*" To us, this was more of an insult than a compliment. Babies are cute. Puppies are cute.

Zachary A. Schaefer Ph.D. & David J. Ponder CISA

We were amateur magicians who had just tricked an entire audience of adults into believing that we made a coin disappear, and they didn't have a clue as to how we did it. And they called us cute? Zach and I stepped aside to figure out what we were doing wrong. Were we not selling it enough? Something else? Then it hit us: we hadn't made any bets. We'd just hoped that people would throw a few bucks into the tip jar on their own free will. I guess the *free will* wasn't free that night, because until we made specific bets with the spectators, we didn't earn a dime. So that is what we did.

We started small, betting people a dollar or two that we could make coins disappear and guess what cards they were holding. To our surprise, once we attached specific monetary values to our tricks, people would not only pay what they owed us but usually throw in a few extra dollars as a tip. We were on our way to becoming professional magicians! Don reassured us that as the night went on we would make more money. At the time we didn't quite understand why, but we also didn't know about the mystical social lubricant called "alcohol." This magical elixir would slowly lower people's ability to make rational, logical, and well-thought-out decisions. In other words, a drunken audience is a great audience for any performer because people want to be entertained, they want mysterious actions to awe them, and they are much more willing to part with their dollars when buzzed.

To a sober man, betting on a magic trick with a grade schooler is a friendly gesture, but after a few beers it becomes a slap in the face, a duel of wits, and who wants to be outwitted by a seventh grader? By the end of the night, we were making $20 bets by preying on the least-sober guests. An easy way to identify who was—or was about to be—the drunkest was to find the guys carrying two or three beer pitchers to get refilled. It was like shooting fish in a barrel. At one point, we made $100 on one trick and received a standing, swaying, and slurring ovation from our intoxicated admirers. Luckily, our first performance took place in Belleville, where kids shoot potato guns, blow things up, shoot off firecrackers, make prank calls, play sports for hours on end, and get into neighborhood water fights. Adults have no access to any of these fun outlets because they would be shunned by the rest of the adult community. So what do many adults in Belleville do for fun? They drink, and drink, and drink some more. Once we discovered that we could exploit this cultural anomaly, we did so with great pride.

    Don typically pulled in $200-$250 in tips when bartending a wedding reception, which he always split with his assistant. On the opening night of *Schonder Magic* at the McCormack Center, Zach and I reeled in an unimaginable $565. To our happy surprise, Don let us keep the entire haul. We had never "earned" that much money in our lives. We were as successful as Siegfried and Roy, only our magic was better, we were funnier, and we didn't get mauled by tigers. To the drunk wedding guests, David Copperfield didn't have anything on us, and from that point forward, the tip jar that Don used when bartending was now labeled *Magic Tip Jar*. In the coming weeks and months, whenever Zach and

I worked wedding receptions, that jar would find itself magically filled by the end of the evening.

Morals of the Story

1. Mystery keeps people interested, engaged, and wanting more.

2. Revealing your secrets decreases the inspiration that people get from your actions.

3. The more alcohol people drink, the more they are willing to give money to seventh-grade magicians.

Chapter 11
Pyramid Schemers

Our eyes opened wide as we walked across the hand-laid brick driveway onto the patterned sidewalk made of stone pavers leading up to one of the largest houses we'd ever seen.

"This, boys, is why you're joining the team representing the world's best long-distance service. This is luxury. Let me ask you a question: Does this look like something you'd want for yourselves someday," said the slick sales manager named Darnell.

We'd already been introduced to the smaller luxuries that other "team members" enjoyed. A nice dinner and a ride in a Range Rover were enough to convince Dave and me that we had to be a part of whatever magical moneymaking machine these guys had. Now, walking up to this mansion, in a town a little over an hour from Belleville, we were sold. Of course, we didn't know the guy who owned the house, and his organization was a level "upstream" from our sponsor Darnell's organization and two levels upstream from what Dave's and mine would be. At least that's how it was described to us as a part of the Excel Communications multi-level marketing structure. Just two levels of separation! We could almost smell the crisp new Benjamins filling our wallets. After a tour of the 5,000-square foot manor, complete with its fairy-tale-themed children's bedrooms, one of which had a two-story slide affixed to a Robin Hood tree house, we couldn't sign the paperwork fast enough.

For our $400 one-time "application fee," we received a nice faux-leather binder with an Excel logo and a bunch of getting-started material. We hit the ground running with the people Darnell had suggested we talk to first: friends and family. After all, wouldn't they want to help us out with starting our business while receiving superior long-distance phone service at a price that was surely cheaper than what they were paying through their current carrier? Imagine our surprise when my own mother, the lovable and always amicable Maureen Schaefer, hit us with a hard dose of reality.

"No, Zachary, I don't want to change my long-distance telephone service. I'm happy with it as it is, and I get one bill through MCI since they provide both my local and long-distance service. I don't want two different bills, and honestly, I just don't want to deal with the hassle of switching to someone new."

"But it's only two short forms to complete, Mom," I pleaded, "and you can clearly see that the five-cent-a-minute rate to Canada is cheaper than the seven cents you're currently paying!"

"I don't call Canada, and I'm not changing my phone service," the woman formerly known as Mom said.

This unwelcome development threw our plans for global phone service domination for a loop. We had no answer for the fact that my Mom did not want two separate bills. We had no answer for the fact that she never called Canada. If getting my own Mom to sign up for the service was this hard, our plan to sign up our extended family, to capture our friends' parents, and to convert every person in the St. Louis Metro East area to Excel long-distance service was going to be nearly impossible.

Even so, we did score a few small victories along the way. Dave's Mom and grandma were pushovers and converted right away, and I can clearly recall eking out by the narrowest of margins a long kitchen-table battle with our good friend Jimmie's stepdad, Randy. We were surprised to win this one, because Randy was a master salesman himself, a smooth-talking, funny, business-savvy man who easily saw through our sales pitch. Looking back, he probably switched his phone service to make his stepson (and his wife) happy. To us, he simply recognized savings, even if it was only two cents a call to Canada.

Another victory came when we convinced our boss at the Belle Clair Fairgrounds to allow us a free table during the weekend flea market, so we could preach the good word of Excel long distance. Despite our best efforts, the "No's" piled up, and the repeated rejections over the course of the month before we decided to throw in the towel made for a difficult life in the business world. Cold-propositioning people at a flea market and trying to get them to come to your booth to discuss their long-distance phone service was an exercise in humility and futility. By the end of the flea market, both Dave and I felt like beggars sitting on the corner asking for change. The word No, when heard a thousand times, can break even the strongest resolve.

Afterward, everything became crystal clear. The warning flags were there to be seen. First there was the fact that Darnell had approached us, at a Borders Bookstore, two 16-year-old high school kids, complete strangers, with an offer to make money. Then there was his Range Rover; it was nice, but I noticed it had over a hundred thousand miles on it. On top of that, to become an Excel "distributor," we'd have to pay that application fee of $400. And the mansion? We saw the guy with the big house exactly once.

Unfortunately, we had let the excitement—and the promise of recurring paychecks for no additional work—get the better of us. As Gary Craig, our current friend and financial advisor, would later say, never invest using emotion.

Fortunately, the fallout wasn't too bad. Our relatives and a couple of our friends' parents ended up with a different long-distance provider, and we were out $400 apiece. Plus, we were forced to concede something that no 16-year-old boy would ever willingly want to admit: our parents were right. Even so, looking back, I can still hear Dad saying the lesson we learned by losing our own money would be worth it. It stung at the time, but in hindsight I know that that $400 didn't go to waste. It didn't simply fund our class to join Excel. It paid for a lifelong course that taught us countless lessons crucial to business, such as how to identify the warning signs of a scam or that in business you have to temper emotions and excitement that well up at the promise

Friendship, LLC

of future money in order to think logically. And it confirmed the age-old adage that if something seems too good to be true, it probably is.

Morals of the Story

1. Be wary of unsolicited money-making offers.

2. Follow your instincts and temper your emotions. Don't let excitement cause you to overlook warning signs.

3. Never trust a man with a Robin Hood tree house in his home.

Chapter 12
RESPONSIBILITY HAPPENS

Like most concepts, responsibility is a subjective term. What one person deems responsible another person might call negligent. Let's say Donnie finally talks his parents into buying him a puppy, but only if he feeds and walks it every day. Donnie of course agrees to this arrangement and begins caring for the pup, cleaning up after it, and walking it every day … for the first month or two. After that, his parents are forced to take over, and soon that puppy is dependent on them because Donnie is now infatuated with playing sports, riding bikes, and chasing girls. Is Donnie acting responsibly? Arguments could be made both ways. But a few key questions can be asked and answered to better understand how and why kids embrace responsibility.

Can you call a child responsible if he or she is being *forced* by a parent or authority figure to be accountable for his or her actions? We don't think so. Parental guidelines, rules, and structures can create a foundation that *fosters* responsibility, but it is up to each individual to own that responsibility. How do kids learn responsibility? We believe they learn to be responsible from watching and listening to their parents, siblings, teachers, and friends' actions and norms. Zach and I both admit that we didn't actively try to become responsible boys or adults—it sort of snuck up on us and just happened.

We had thought, similarly to those wise words "shit happens," that *responsibility happens*. But we came to realize that a sense of responsibility does not automatically develop within children but slowly and subtly creeps into their actions as a result of their upbringing and guidance. It may be difficult to pick a particular event that teaches a young person to be responsible, say, for his or her actions or property, but in the following three chapters we offer several experiences from our own lives that accomplished four things: (a) they taught Zach and me important lessons about the role of the almighty dollar, like the value of money in our society and how hard it is to earn and keep it; (b) they taught us that to buy and own luxurious items you must save money and take care of the items post-purchase; (c) they demonstrated that many people end up letting their things own them by putting the things ahead of their relationships; and (d) they showed us that money is a steering mechanism, a means to an end, and for us, that *end* is to lead fulfilling lives surrounded by friends and family and to leave the world a better place than when we found it.

Chapter 13
Boating, Bonding and Cleaning

"Remember, boys: thumbs up for faster, thumbs down for slower, and hand across the throat for stopping." These were the directions Art gave us when Dave and I would go tubing on the Kaskaskia River in southern Illinois, but we never used the thumbs-down or stopping gestures because we always wanted to go faster, so that Art would create more wake and we would be thrown ever higher off the choppy water. In the early 1990s, the Ponders had purchased a fun summer "toy," a brand-new turquoise Ebbtide Campione 182 speedboat, a heckuva plaything because it could easily reach 45 miles an hour while towing two tubes, each tube holding two kids.

The Kaskaskia excursions gave us so many happy memories because the Ebbtide could accommodate everyone from both our families. We would be out on the river early in the morning and stay tubing till dusk. Because the days were long, Mary, Dave's mom, always packed picnic lunches that we would eat while anchored near a sandbar so that we could all swim.

Looking back at our tubing and boogie-boarding adventures as a 30-year-old expectant father, I have to admit they were crazy dangerous, mainly because we were being pulled through fast, murky water at high speeds and slamming against four-foot waves that threw us several feet in the air. I remember one time, after 15 minutes of nonstop tubing at high speed, we were thrown off the tube and went airborne for several seconds before crashing back into the choppy, muddy current. It seemed the Ebbtide was going 100 miles an hour, but the danger never entered our minds. When Dave and I were crammed into the round rubber chambers of death, adult life jackets hanging awkwardly off our skinny bodies, we had no fear. In our minds, everyone came to the river to watch our water show and be awed by a couple of grade schoolers who had overcome their fears.

We had a few options at our disposal to take full advantage of the boat's horsepower. For example, we would ride together in a single tube because the extra weight meant we would get thrown higher into the air. Plus, when Art would take long lateral turns, the rope would go slightly slack, then snap back and jerk the tube through the water, our white-knuckled hands clinging to the handles for dear life. Once, we were holding on so tightly during a particularly raucous ride that one of the handles ripped completely off, but instead of jumping ship Zach and I rode it out for another five minutes.

When entering the rainbow-colored inner tube, we took the ride as a personal challenge, like astronauts training for a shuttle launch. The goal was to stay on for as long as possible, and the only way we ended our tubing experiences was flying off of them—never because we used the "kill the engine" gesture. That was for girls.

To add to our fun, we created a competition where Dave and I would tube separately and see who could stay on the longest. These battles were fun because the tubes would ram into each other, sometimes causing them to jump over the one another, so you had to make sure you ducked during the "tube hops" if you didn't want to lose your head.

In the last few summers of grade school and the first few summers of high school, our families spent countless weekends on the Kaskaskia, eating salami-and-mustard sandwiches, munching on Cheetos, and drinking case upon case of soda—this of course was before our parents knew how terrible drinking sugar water was for your health. As soon as Art thought we were old enough—we'd just started high school—he began letting us help him back the boat into the water and later load it onto the trailer. He let us do this because we were taller than Mary and so could see better when backing up the trailer. One of us would get to back the Dodge Dakota pickup with its boat trailer into the water while the other manned the boat itself. These experiences, which made us feel like adults (and occurred under strict supervision), only happened when there weren't other boaters putting their vessels in the water.

After years on the river under his father's supervision, Dave finally persuaded Art to let us take the boat out on our own, even letting us include our girlfriends. Dave was 16 and had his driver's license. Art knew he was a responsible driver because Art had taught both Dave and me to drive a manual transmission Honda Civic on the back roads of Millstadt, Illinois when we were 14. By the time we turned 16, we had two years of driving experience under our belts and were completely confident in our abilities behind the wheel.

Beyond the fun we had on the water, the sense of pride and the ego-enhancing emotions we got from driving the boat and truck, Dave and I quickly learned that the pursuit of fun is not always fun. What were supposed to be days of pleasure—and were till the moment we had to pull the boat out of the water—quickly morphed into an atmosphere of concentration-camp misery orchestrated by the lead officer, Dave's dad, who could uncannily jump from warm-hearted father to tough-as-nails drill sergeant.

Art, understandably, wanted to ensure that his new toy would last a long time, so upon pulling the boat out of the water, all passengers would spend literally two hours cleaning every inch of it from stem to stern, and I do mean every inch. Art should have owned stock in Proctor & Gamble because he used every cleaning product known to man: tire cleaner for the tires, chrome cleaner for the trim, glass cleaner for the windows, and chamois, soft cloths, towels, squeegees, and sponges for everything else.

Art also brought his shop vac, and I remember his constantly saying, "I don't want to see one drop of water on this boat, boys." I'd think, "What is he talking about? This is a boat; it's made to go in the water." Mary would try to be the voice of reason and ask Art to go easy on us, sensibly pointing out that a few drops of water would not rot out the bottom of a fiberglass boat. But that was nothing less than heresy to Art, and Mary's advice went in one ear and out the other. "If these boys want to enjoy this boat, they'll follow my rules," he said. Ah, invoking the "fallacy of authority" to coerce us to fulfill his wishes. "Why do they have to do this," an observer might ask. "Because I said so, it's my boat, I bought it, and they're my kids," would have been Art's response.

So every time we used that boat we spent hours cleaning it as if had been out to sea for months. Later, when Art sold the boat, he said he was astonished at how well it had held its value. So all the scrubbing, vacuuming, and obsessive attention to detail did pay off—in many ways, as it turned out. It helped Art keep some coin in his pocket, it showed Dave and me the importance of taking care of your "stuff" and taking pride in what you own, and it taught us to not obsess over our possessions or they'll end up owning you. Proving the point that lessons are learned throughout life, Art recently admitted that he "may have" gone overboard with the boat cleaning. Dave and I should have given Art a "cut the cleaning" gesture after 30 minutes of vacuuming the bottom of that Ebbtide, flat on our backs on the burning asphalt, but even as self-absorbed teenagers we understood his fanatical attention to his pride and joy. He wanted it in excellent condition so that our families could enjoy it in the future.

Morals of the Story

1. Fear can be a negative and positive emotion. You can use it as motivation to accomplish a goal.

2. Take care of your possessions but don't let them possess you.

3. Coercive responsibility isn't effective in the long run.

4. If you're serious about being responsible, don't be surprised if your hours of fun are followed by hours of work.

5. When you're towing two young men in a high-powered speedboat on a dirty river, give them all they can handle ... even if the handles tear off.

Chapter 14
Guinea Pig City

Whoever coined the saying "breeding like rabbits" must have never owned guinea pigs. The duplex that Dad moved into across the street from the Ponders had a strict no-pets policy, so the possibility of getting a dog was out of the question. Josh and I wanted to have a pet at Dad's place, which was a two level duplex with a detached garage. We had convinced Mom to buy us a Dalmatian named sugar, so now it was Dad's turn to up the ante. Dad's solution? Guinea pigs. Mind you, neither Josh nor I knew what a guinea pig was when he brought them home. Dave and I vividly remember my Dad walking through the door with the four furry additions to the Schaefer family. The woman at the pet store had guaranteed him that all of the rodents were male, which was critical because apparently guinea pigs are lusty critters and are only too happy to breed with their offspring, thereby quickly increasing the size of their flock. Dad didn't want this to occur, so he double-checked with the woman to ensure his new adoptees were all male, which, as I say, she insisted they were.

Dave and I remember seeing the tiny animals scurrying around the cardboard box that they'd come home in. Dad had sprinkled cedar chips on the bottom of the box because the little buggers love to burrow down to hide themselves from potential threats. The largest of the new family members was all black, and we named him Todd after a good friend of ours named Todd Lanterman, who was probably the funniest improv person we'd ever met. In addition to Todd, there was an all-brown guinea with a large white spot on its back we named Butch, an albino guinea we named Whitey and the smallest guinea of the pack we called—what else—Tiny.

It was amazing how big the guinea pigs got in the first month we had them. They each probably tripled in size, but there was something odd about Todd. It was as if he were on GGH, guinea growth hormone; he was literally three times the size of the other guineas. He looked as if he'd wandered into a sewer and learned the "secret of the ooze" from the Ninja Turtles. Todd was not only bigger than the others, he was eager to exert his dominance. He chased the other guineas away from the food, he bit them, and he insisted on sleeping in his own "room." Dad had constructed a nice guinea pig condo out of some cardboard boxes, with separate rooms, a workout facility with hamster balls and climbing tunnels, a garage with one of my an old monster truck toys inside, and a kitchen where the guineas could eat. Todd quickly claimed the master bedroom where he patrolled his turf to keep the other guineas from trespassing. Todd was a badass and knew it. The other guineas were at his mercy.

One day, Josh, Dave, and I went to feed the four boys when we noticed something odd. There was a

Friendship, LLC

large pile of wood chips stacked to one side of Butch's bedroom, and it appeared to be moving. When we brushed some of the chips away, we were shocked to discover six baby guinea pigs! Wow. We had just witnessed the miracle of life, and possibly a biological aberration. How could four male guineas have made six babies? We couldn't answer this, but my Dad sure could. He called that woman at the pet shop, and from the tone of the conversation, I could tell she wouldn't be guaranteeing the sex of guinea pigs to her customers again anytime soon. Butch was a woman.

Although Dad was upset, he could see how excited we were about the babies, so he let us keep them. He did, however, try to inspect the sex of each guinea pig, after which he built separate living quarters for what he believed to be the males and the females. It was like summer camp: the boys on one side of the lake and the girls on the other. But if you've ever seen a summer camp movie, you know that come nightfall, the boys always canoe across the lake to hang with the girls. Guinea pigs are no different. Within a week of Dad's construction project, the males had literally chewed through the apartment walls to meet (mate with) the females. After a few short—very short—months of owning four "male" guinea pigs, we now owned a staggering total of 26! We figured out that Todd had a lot to do with this population explosion because he would not stop gyrating on the backs of the other guineas. "Todd, what're you doing to Butch?" we exclaimed. Being grade school children, we probably romanticized Todd, thinking of him wining and dining the females in the flock when in reality he was more like the Genghis Khan of guineas, taking what he wanted, when he wanted, and with force. Todd flirted dangerously with persistent advancement and rape. Let's just say that Todd didn't take no for an answer.

After just a few months of illegal pet ownership, we were now up to over 50 guinea pigs. *Fifty!* The sheer quantity, coupled with the range of barnyard smells wafting up the stairs, persuaded Dad to build the guineas a suburban community in our detached garage. Oh, how I wish we had photos of that monstrosity. I remember it took Don an entire weekend to build this complex, which had multiple levels, including a shopping area with guinea-appropriate toys, restaurants, and several gyms. By the time we moved the guineas to the garage, there were *54* of them. Then tragedy struck Guinea City.

One of the local neighborhood kids learned of Guinea City, and unfortunately, this kid, whom we'll call Richard, came from a broken home. His father was an alcoholic in a wheelchair, his mother had abandoned the family for another man, and Richard and his younger brother had been left to fend for themselves. Richard, who was small for his age, didn't shower on a regular basis and lacked understanding of such social norms as reciprocity and sharing. He wasn't an athlete, wasn't particularly bright, and was always yelling obscenities at the other neighborhood kids and then running home to escape beatings. In short, Richard was an asshole. Most of us looked for a reason to get into a scuffle with this guy, but an opportunity rarely present-

Friendship, LLC

ed itself. Plus, Dave and I wouldn't fight him because he was so much smaller and younger than we were, but each of us did have a younger brother who salivated at the chance to teach Richard a lesson. With the development of Guinea City in our garage, the chance presented itself.

One of our neighbors witnessed Richard and his brother entering the garage and emerging with a bag, which the brothers then slammed against the outside garage wall before dropping it and running off. It turns out that these little bastards had captured a few of the guineas and bludgeoned them to death just for the sadistic thrill of it. If Dave and I learned one thing growing up, it was never to hurt defenseless animals or children. We also were taught what justice meant, and we believed that it meant turning a wrong into a right. A grittier, more honest, and more fulfilling form of justice is called revenge. We learned what revenge meant soon after our neighbor came forward to point out who had perpetrated this wicked deed. We were all heartbroken, and when my father arrived home and learned of the story, he marched directly over to the boys' house and told their father what he thought of his sons.

Soon enough, Dave, Josh, Justin and I came up with a plan of our own and met to strategize how to move forward. We couldn't just break into Richard's house and beat him up at the foot of his father's wheelchair. While we knew those cowards wouldn't leave the house unless they had to, we had one thing they didn't have: patience. At some point they would have to walk to school, since their father couldn't drive them, so we would take them by surprise early one morning. Dave and I weren't going to fight them, but we could at least help catch them and force his brother to watch Richard receive his comeuppance. Dave's brother Justin, who is now a member of the Navy Special Forces, was also too young and small to participate in the beating, so it was left to my brother Josh, who had been known to choke me out when wrestling almost to the point of unconsciousness.

Dad had installed a trapeze in our backyard when Josh and I were children, and it gave Josh an outlet to show how freakishly strong he was for a little guy, and that didn't change as he grew. For Richard-payback day, Josh and I convinced Dad to let us stay the night at Dave's and then told Mary that we—Dave, Josh, Justin, and I—were going to walk to school together. We got up extra early and conducted a stake-out, each of us strategically placed around the house and out of sight, to surveil the animal killers. Then it happened. The back door came open very slowly, and Dave saw Richard peeking through the screen, looking for his rivals. Not seeing us, Richard and his brother took off running toward their school, a block away. Since we couldn't pound them in their front yard, we had to chase them to a neutral site. Which we did.

Before Richard and his brother knew what was happening, Dave was chasing them from behind, I was coming at them from in front, and Justin was joining the fray from the right; they didn't even see Josh barreling in from the left. It was priceless. You could smell their fear. As we funneled them toward Justin, who was the smallest of the bunch, Josh took a page out of pro wrestler Bill Goldberg's book and landed a diving spear directly into Richard's side. The felon was blindsided and dropped like a ton of bricks. For a fight between a fourth grader (Josh) and a sixth grader, it was pretty violent. Through his tears, Josh unleashed such a flurry of punches, kicks, elbows, and choke holds on Richard that Dave and I finally had to pull him off, and we were both scared that Josh would accidentally hurt us in his blind rage. We thought he might kill Richard if we didn't end the fight, and perhaps he might have. The collective adrenaline pumping through our bodies could have killed a grown man. Even today, neither Dave nor I will fight Josh, his quiet rage and polite persona masking the raw vengeance that he is willing to unleash on people who deserve it. Nor would we mess with Justin, who is now a specially trained lethal weapon.

We don't know if it was because of this incident, but within six months of "Josh Justice," Richard's family moved out of the neighborhood. Even though we felt that we had done the right thing by the deceased inhabitants of Guinea City, we couldn't let matters end there and allow our surviving furry friends to continue to live in potential peril, so we relocated their entire suburb back to Dad's basement. This gentrification came at great cost, however: realizing that the care and maintenance of the animals had grown beyond our scope, we convinced Dad to give them away, making sure they went to good homes. Although we screened would-be owners, Dad gave up on the sex-segregated dormitories of before and allowed males and females to "intermingle," which led to another population explosion—to an unfathomable *72* pigs. We managed to come up with names for over half of them, and Todd, who had escaped the massacre, was elected mayor.

In the final few weeks, the economy of Guinea City took a turn for the worse. The residents knew that their relatives and neighbors were being evacuated from the city, and ghettos developed where guinea gangs caused trouble, fought smaller guineas, and stole food. Guinea families quit dropping in on the different restaurants (feeding areas), quit using the gyms (where the exercise toys were located), and stopped visiting the upper level of the complex (because that was where the ghettos were situated).

By the time we gave Todd away, we had learned a lot about responsibility, loss, and settling of scores. Although we are not advocating violence to solve one's problems, in this particular instance it did work. It made us happy, and it taught Richard a lesson. We also learned the importance of being able to biologically distinguish between males and females within the rodent kingdom. A few years later Dad bought Josh and I a floppy-eared rabbit, but only one to ensure population control. Dad always said that he was proud of the way we handled the situation, perhaps because we had misinformed him that we had a stern talk with Richard about the incident. But until this book, we never told him (or anyone) that we were the ones who had orchestrated the capture and beating of the perpetrators of the Guinea City Massacre.

Morals of the Story

1. Even when people are trying to be honest, they can still be incorrect.

2. Vengeance is not morally popular, but it is an unrobed form of justice that rights a wrong.

3. Cleaning the feces of 72 animals, no matter how small, can easily dissuade whiny kids from pet ownership.

Chapter 15
Boxing, Brawling and Bravery

One evening, when I was 11 and Zach was 10, Don took us to watch some kickboxing matches at Fischer's restaurant in Belleville. Don had always hinted to Zach and me that martial arts were a good way to learn discipline, and he offered to enroll us in martial-arts classes on several occasions. Don had been given free tickets to the matches by his brother-in-law, Uncle Joe. Joe, owner of Boeving's Barber Shop in Belleville, always had the inside scoop on the goings on around town and was usually able to get his hands on event tickets. Whether it was because he had been given the tickets, or whether he was trying to pique our interest in martial arts, Don took us to the kickboxing matches for what would turn out to be one of the most exciting experiences of our childhood.

The evening of the fights, the restaurant had been converted into a boxing arena, with a ring set up in the middle, the tables cleared out (except for the front row where the judges sat), and the chairs arranged to face the action. I'm sure if we looked at the set-up today it would seem like the amateur boxing venue that it was, but to a couple of 11-year-old kids, the crowd and the crystal chandeliers made the room the definition of a big-time setting. It might as well have been the Roman Coliseum.

The air was electric, and with every leg kick absorbed, every stomach punch landed, and every pitcher of beer chugged, the crowd became more rowdy. Although I don't remember the results or the participants of the early matches, I can clearly recall the American flag pants worn by the defending champion during the main event. To Zach and I, this guy was a real American hero, and after we agreed to root for the red, white, and blue, we gave each other an enthusiastic high five at the sound of the opening bell.

The action started strong, and it was clear that the challenger was there to fight. This wasn't going to be a cakewalk for Captain America, and by the end of round two both fighters had retreated to their corners sporting a cut on their face and a swollen lip. Then, shortly into round three, it happened. Quickly but deliberately, the challenger delivered a sharp elbow to the nose of the champion. The crowd erupted with a deafening clamor, and all that could be heard was a chorus of boos. Landing a flying elbow to the face was illegal, a cheap shot if ever there was one.

The crowd wanted the referee to penalize the illegal move but he didn't—in fact, he didn't flinch. This was not what the crowd wanted. What Zach and I heard next was as profane as any string of curse words a drunk ever spoke. We spun around and stared at the pretty thirty-something-year-old-blonde obscenity artist. Impressed, Zach and I looked at each other, eyes wide, and slammed another animated high five.

"Awesome!" Zach said over the commotion.

Don's take was different. "Watch your mouth, lady! We've got children here."

"Shut up and sit down, old man," her companion shouted. He was a kick boxer who'd made his way into the audience after the conclusion of his earlier fight, which he'd lost.

Don was never one to back down. He stood up and pointed at the man, who was slouched in his chair with a beer in his hand. "I've seen what you've got, but you don't know what I've got!" This was Don Schaefer justice: raw, honest, and courageous; he wasn't going to be pushed around.

Shortly after Don uttered his fighting words, the first half-full airborne pitcher of beer appeared in my peripheral vision. If it was aimed at either party now engaged in the verbal battle, it missed its mark by a mile, slamming into the man-perm of a curly-haired innocent bystander. The second projectile was an empty glass, and the peak of its flight signaled the start of a frenzy of flying fists and beverage containers.

The fight in the ring was stopped due to—or in deference to—the action in the audience. Within no time, Don had switched his attention to getting Zach and me out of harm's way, which meant, ironically, into the ring itself. It couldn't have ended better (for us). Being in the ring, Zach and I had a front-row seat, as it were, for the arrest of the blonde and her amateur kickboxing boyfriend. Even better, we got the autograph of the flag pants champ, who shadow-boxed us through a couple of punches and kicks for our trouble. It was the best free lesson we had ever received.

I returned home having learned that fighting usually ends badly for those involved and with new respect and admiration for Don. That evening, he stood up for what was right and wasn't afraid to tell people that their behavior was unacceptable. After being threatened, by a fighter, no less, Don was unfazed and was willing to put his well-being on the line to protect his kids. In the end, the champion kept his belt, the drunks ended up in the back of a cop car, and we had an exhilarating experience to add to our growth curve. The good guys won, and though Captain America was there, Don emerged as the hero of the evening.

Morals of the Story

1. Be assertive and stand up for what you believe in.

2. Pay attention to your surroundings and respect those around you.

3. Never challenge an old man to a fight.

Chapter 16
Reflections and Perspectives

Dave's Perspective

We're all trying to find happiness and figure out our place in the world. Many people reason that their friends, profession, hobbies, and interests have naturally fallen into their current lives. When looking at upper crust outliers such as royalty, celebrities, and heirs to family fortunes, and downtrodden outliers like disabled homeless people who lack a social support structure, one cannot deny that *chance* has a considerable impact. For those of us closer to the middle of the bell curve, which is the majority of folks, serendipity's impact on our lives can be amplified or minimized by our actions. The place we live and the people we interact with heavily influence us. While it's easy to see the smaller, more direct impacts of daily choices (Do I read a book or watch the football game with friends? Do I stay in to finish some work or do I go out to dinner? Do I join a softball league or spend more time at the gym?), it's harder to draw the connection between decisions and their larger, indirect consequences (Do I stay in my hometown or move to the big city? Which course of study should I choose? Should I ask her to dinner or not?). It's easy to look at the biggest parts of our daily lives and forget how they appeared. For most of us, our friends, profession, hobbies, and interests are chosen. That is, we socially construct our lives with the choices we make on a daily basis. One of the most important choices we make is the people we surround ourselves with.

As I look at the biggest parts of my life today, most of them have been influenced by my relationship with Zach Schaefer. The person that I am today has been built on the foundation of our shared childhood and young adult experiences. My profession is largely a result of the opportunities cultivated by attending St. Louis University, a decision heavily influenced by Zach. My desire to pursue business opportunities outside of my daily job was encouraged by Zach, and he's served as an example for me to follow (and try to keep up with). He even introduced me to my wife!

Over the course of our lives, our strengths and weaknesses as human beings have complemented one another. The strengths that I've co-developed with Zach include generating ideas and improving processes. Perhaps due to risk aversion, or perhaps because I had moved onto a new idea by the time I gained any traction, early in life I struggled with producing some of the things I dreamed up. Zach, on the other hand, always has had a laser focus and an unstoppable drive. Observing Zach's strengths helped me become more self-reflective and helped me recognize and work on some of my weaknesses. When left unchecked, I have a natural tendency for procrastination, conservative

Friendship, LLC

action, and safety that can lead to stagnation through comfort. Knowing Zach has helped me recognize those attributes, and often times he has served as a direct catalyst for taking a risk, an inspiration for branching out, and as a motivator to work harder. I've improved my ability to achieve simply by knowing Zach.

The experiences I've shared with Zach give us a common understanding that allows us to discuss ideas without having to first lay the groundwork of context in which most personal and professional interactions become bogged down. A theme in our recent conversations has been coping with the negative viewpoints that come with age. For some reason, there is a correlation between (a) becoming older and more informed with (b) developing a lethargic negativity. For instance, most older men would rather complain than solve problems. That *is* a problem. As stated by Robert Anton Wilson, a critical thinker who Zach told me about, negativity and pessimism are crippling. Pessimists spend all of their time complaining and rarely get anything done. Keeping an *alive* mind is one of the harder things to do in life. Positivity drives action. Action arises from need. But before actions can positively change things, you should try to identify and understand the needs of social groups outside of your comfort zone. Empathy, and perhaps to a greater extent "understanding without compassion," allows for the emergence of useful contrarian ideas. It's important to "play with" contrarian ideas because ideas show opportunity, opportunity shows hope, and hope breeds happiness. Falling back into pessimism is all too easy; informed optimism is an achievement in itself. Whenever the grind of daily life starts to wear me down, Zach sends me a reminder, a verbal slap in the face. Wake up! Think positively! Identify opportunity! Take action!

One fateful evening, I met Zach when my family decided to grab some flashlights and help his family find a lost set of keys in their front yard. I'm not even sure if I was involved in the decision, but over the past 20 plus years I've made many decisions that have kept Zach as an important part of my life. When I look around at all of the good people and things that surround me, when I recognize how happy I am today, and when I get excited thinking about all of my future opportunities, I credit much to Zach.

The next time you're able to slow down and analyze the things in your life and how they impact your happiness, try to look past the direct impacts of your recent decisions. Identify your major influences and find those that are a force of good in your life. Look back farther and try to identify their origins. Have you found your Zach Schaefer?

Zach's Perspective

I learned a lot growing up with Dave Ponder. He helped me become the person I am today, and most of my better qualities are a reflection of the impact that he had, and continues to have, on my life. My personal philosophy consists of five core principles that Dave helped me develop: persistence, balance, spontaneity, self-confidence, and passion. Getting into and out of trouble with Dave as boys and young men, being privileged to stand by his side as he beat cancer twice, and simply observing his outlook on life have influenced my thoughts, actions, and values in more ways than I can describe.

Dave is still helping me move from reactionary self-confidence, the feeling of having to prove myself to others, to feelings of authentic self-confidence without arrogance. Dave and I both strive for balance in our professional and personal lives as we continually set goals, and, when we reach them, set new ones. We challenge each other to leave a mark on the planet and in the lives of the people we encounter on it. Learning about the world through travel, seeking new experiences, meeting new people, and having a zest for life will always be a core component of my identity. I have always had a passion for life but have never had a "calling," that one profession or craft I felt I was put on this planet to pursue. I am finally beginning to accept rather than regret or change this fact, and Dave is the person who taught me how to make peace with it.

Letting go is scary for a control freak like myself, but it can also be thrillingly liberating and self-revealing. Consciously trying to go with the flow rather than control the current has led to several positive professional transformations in my life. Through a series of serendipitous opportunities and the resolve to keep an open mind, I have had the pleasure of being exposed to thousands of interesting people, ideas, and places. But all of my travels and knowledge are worthless without friends, family, and colleagues to share them with. Because I believe that new ideas emerge as technology, communication, medicine, law, and a variety of other fields intersect, I know that my current "beliefs" will change over time. In fact, I try not to have beliefs at all—I prefer ideas. Ideas are more malleable, more flexible, and more playful. They are less permanent and can be shifted around. Beliefs are static, even in the face of contradictory evidence. My education (what you remember once you forget everything that you learned in school, as the truism goes), is tied to my friendship and intellectual development with Dave.

That development, including teaching, research, mediating, and starting a consulting business, has benefitted in countless ways from my relationship with Dave. I have learned to be more patient with students and clients, to ask thoughtful questions rather than look to be the expert, and to make changes based on other people's responses. Although I keep high professional expectations for myself, Dave has helped me step back and value my accomplishments. It has always been difficult for me to stay in the moment, to appreciate the recognition that I have earned, but Dave has showed me that it's acceptable to be proud of what you do and of who you are.

Not only did Dave teach me to be proud of what I've accomplished, he also served a socio-psychological function in my life. To date, he has helped me avoid catching OMS—Old Man Syndrome—that disease exhibited in older men who believe that what they know is absolute knowledge, and who then impose that knowledge on others by treating other people's experiences and views as inferior. Dave has been my antidote to OMS, and I attribute my endless curiosity and willingness to continue learning to my lifelong friendship with Dave.

At times our friendship still resembles that of two 10-year-old boys shooting potato guns and making prank calls without caring what others think of us. To this day, we take jokes way past the line of social acceptability, and as we laugh ourselves to tears, we still couldn't care less what others think. We're proud that we've kept our childlike inquisitiveness, that we continue to seek new experiences, and that we share our adventures with diverse groups of people. But our relationship has also become more professional, more business-like, and more intellectual. We think and talk about how new technologies and innovations can positively and negatively affect our lives, we laugh at the current crop of politicians, we think of new inventions that can make life more comfortable, we contemplate the purpose of consciousness, and we have combined our strengths to start our own businesses. If it weren't for Dave (and Gary Craig), my consulting business would never have gotten off the ground. Gary taught me the business side of things and to be bold; Dave taught me how to form lasting relationships with clients and how to cultivate entrepreneurial thinking. One idea that is always in the back of my mind is that if Dave can successfully battle the most life-threatening human disease, twice, I can apply my knowledge of communication and conflict to improve organizational life, even if it makes me a little uncomfortable when trying to "sell" the business. Dave's courage puts my life's struggles and goals into perspective.

Being brutally honest with one another and having the willingness to challenge each other to become better people are the reasons our friendship has lasted this long. If everyone had a Dave Ponder in their life, the world would be a more empathetic, positive, and productive place. I am honored and lucky to have met a person who inspires me to soar like an eagle rather than gobble like a turkey.

Made in the USA
Charleston, SC
20 January 2013